EVERY DAY WITH ANDREW MURRAY

Every Day with Andrew Murray

Six Months of Devotional Readings

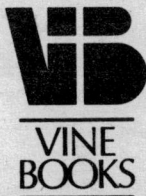

VINE BOOKS

Servant Publications
Ann Arbor, Michigan

This revised edition copyright © 1986 by Servant
Publications
All rights reserved.

Vine Books is an imprint of Servant Publications
especially designed to serve Evangelical Christians

Published by Servant Books
P.O. Box 8617
Ann Arbor, Michigan 48107

86 87 88 89 90 91 10 9 8 7 6 5 4 3 2 1

Printed in the United States of America
ISBN 0-89283-302-5

Introduction

THE MORE I THINK OF AND PRAY about the state of Christianity in this country (South Africa) and all over the world, the more convinced I become that the low state of the spiritual life of Christians is due to the fact that they do not realize that the aim and object of conversion is to bring the soul, even here on earth, to a daily fellowship with the Father in heaven. When this truth has been accepted, the believer will perceive how indispensable it is to the spiritual life of a Christian, to take time each day with God's Word and in prayer, and to wait upon him to reveal his presence and his love.

But how can Christians be taught this lesson, and live in obedience to it? They must first be convinced of the great necessity of daily fellowship with God. They must be brought to realize that it is not enough at conversion to accept forgiveness of sins or even to surrender themselves to God. That is only a beginning. The young believer must understand that he has no power of his own to maintain his spiritual life. No, he needs each day to receive new grace from heaven through communion with the Lord Jesus. This cannot be obtained by a hasty prayer or a superficial reading of a few verses from God's Word. He must take time quietly and deliberately to come into God's presence, to experience his own weakness and his need, and to wait upon God to renew the heavenly light and life in his heart through the Holy Spirit. Then he may rightly expect to be kept by the power of Christ throughout the day and all its temptations.

The purpose of this book is to help Christians to see the absolute necessity of fellowship with the Lord Jesus. Without this, the joy and power of God's Holy Spirit in daily life cannot be experienced. Many of God's children long for a better life, but do not realize the necessity of daily allowing God to renew and sanctify their lives through his Spirit.

Meditate on this thought: The feeble state of my spiritual life is mainly due to the lack of time day by day in fellowship with God. New life would dawn in many Christians as a result of time spent in prayer alone with God.

If you find a blessing in reading this book, please share the blessing with others. If you accept its message—that the Lord Jesus will from day to day grant you his presence and love—pass it on to others. However weak and impotent you may feel, your faith will be strengthened as you help others to realize the need of fellowship with Jesus daily.

As we consider the need of the Church and of all those around us, as we consider the extension of God's kingdom, help find volunteers who, as true soldiers of the cross, will persevere continually in prayer, until God pours out his blessing upon us.

Your servant in the love of Christ and in prayer.

Andrew Murray

Month One

1 Our inner nature is being renewed every day. (2 Cor 4:16)

There is one lesson that all young Christians should learn, namely this: the absolute necessity of fellowship with Jesus each day. This lesson is not always taught at the beginning of the Christian life, nor is it always understood by the young convert. He should realize that the grace he has received—the forgiveness of sins, acceptance as God's child, joy in the Holy Spirit, can only be preserved by daily renewal in fellowship with Jesus Christ himself.

Many Christians backslide because this truth is not clearly taught. They are unable to stand against the temptations of the world and of their old nature. They strive to do their best to fight against sin and to serve God, but they have no strength. They have never really grasped the secret: Every day, the Lord Jesus will continue his work in me. But on one condition: I must give him *time* each day to impart his love and his grace. Time alone with the Lord Jesus each day is the indispensable condition of growth and power.

Read Matthew 11:25-30. Listen to Christ's word: "Come to me, all who labor and are heavy laden, and I will give you rest." The Lord will teach us just how gentle and humble he is. Bow before him, tell him that you long for him and his love, and he will let his love rest on you. This thought is not only for young Christians, but for all who love the Lord.

This book is intended to help those who desire to live this life of fellowship with Christ. I will try to put the message as clearly, as lovingly, as urgently as possible. For Christ's sake and in order to please him, and for my own sake and to enable me to enjoy this blessed experience each day, I will learn the lesson: to spend time each day, without exception, in fellowship with my Lord. So will the inner man be renewed from day to day.

2 Fellowship with God
He who loves me will be loved by my Father. (Jn 14:21)

The Three Persons in the Godhead are the Father, the Son, and the Holy Spirit. Each one knows himself as different from the others. God desires to reveal himself as a Person. Each one of us is an individual, knowing himself as distinct from others and standing in certain relations to others. God will reveal himself to us as a Person, and it is our holy calling to enter into fellowship with him.

God greatly desires this fellowship with man, but sin has come between man and his God. Even in the Christian, who thinks he knows God, there is often great ignorance and even indifference to this personal relationship of love to God.

People believe that at conversion their sins are forgiven, that God accepts them so that they may go to heaven, and that they should try to do God's will. But the idea is strange to them that even as a father and his child on earth have pleasure in communing with each other, so they may and must each day have this fellowship with God.

God gave his Son Jesus to bring us to himself. But this is only possible when we live in close fellowship with Jesus Christ. Our relationship to Christ rests on his deep, tender love for us. We are not able by ourselves to render him this love, but the Holy Spirit will do the work in us. For this we need to separate ourselves each day from the world and turn in faith to the Lord Jesus, that he may pour his love into our hearts and fill us with a great love for him.

Meditate quietly on this thought. Read the words of Christ in John 14:21: "He who loves me will be loved by my

Father, and I will love him and manifest myself to him." Take time to believe in this personal fellowship. Tell him of your love. Say to him, "Lord, you have loved me dearly; I earnestly desire to love you above all else."

3 Jesus
You shall call his name Jesus, for he will save his people from their sins. (Mt 1:21)

Because the Lord Jesus was a person, he had his own individual name. His mother, his disciples, all his friends called him by this name—Jesus. But they probably thought little of what that name meant. And how little do the majority of Christians know what a treasure is contained in that name. "Jesus"—"He will save his people from their sins."

Many think of his death on the cross, they think of his work in heaven as Intercessor. But do they, or do we, realize that he is a living Person in heaven, who thinks of us each day, and longs to reveal himself? And he desires us to daily bring him our love and adoration.

Christians pray to Christ to save them from their sins, but they know very little how this work is done. The living Christ reveals himself to us, and through the power of his love the love of sin is expelled. It is through *personal fellowship with him* that Jesus saves us from our sins. I must come as an individual, with my heart and all the sin that is in it, to Jesus as an almighty personal Savior, in whom God's holiness dwells. And as he and I commune together in the expression of mutual love and desire, by the work of his Holy Spirit in my heart his love will expel and conquer all the sin.

Learn the blessedness of finding in daily fellowship with Jesus the secret of happiness and holiness. Your heart will long for the hour of prayer as the best hour of the day. As you learn to go apart with him each day, you will experience his presence with you, enabling you all through the day to love him, to serve him, and to walk in his ways. Through this unbroken fellowship you will learn the secret of the power of a truly godly life.

4 The Inner Chamber
When thou prayest, enter into thine inner chamber. (Mt 6:6)

Have you ever thought about what a wonderful privilege it is that every one each day and each hour of the day has the liberty of asking God to meet him in the inner chamber, "his room," and to hear what he has to say? We would think that every Christian would use such a privilege gladly and faithfully.

"When thou prayest, enter into thine inner chamber and pray to your Father who is in secret." That means two things. Shut the world out, withdraw from all worldly thoughts and concerns, and shut yourself in alone with God, to pray to him in secret. Let this be your chief object in prayer, to realize the presence of your heavenly Father. Let your watchword be: alone with God.

This is only the beginning. I must take time to realize his presence with me. I must pray to my Father who sees in secret, in the full assurance that he knows how I long for his help and guidance, and that he will incline his ear to me.

Then follows the great promise: "Your Father who sees in secret will reward you." My Father will see to it that my prayer is not in vain. All through the occupations of a busy day, the answer to my prayer will be granted. Prayer in secret will be followed by the secret working of God in my heart.

As the Lord Jesus has promised us his presence and shown us the way to the inner chamber, he will assuredly be with us to teach us to pray. It is through him that we have access to the Father. Be childlike and trustful in your fellowship with Christ. Confess each sin, bring your every need. Offer your prayer to the Father in the name of Christ. Prayer in fellowship with Jesus cannot be in vain.

5 Faith
Only believe. (Mk 5:36)

When we are alone in the inner chamber we must send up our petitions implicitly in the love of God and in the power of the Lord Jesus. Ask yourself this question: Is my heart full of a great and steadfast faith in God's love? If this is not the case, do not begin to pray at once. Faith does not come of itself. Consider quietly how impossible it is for God to lie. He is ready with infinite love to bless you. Take some text of Scripture in which God's power and faithfulness and love are revealed. Appropriate the words and say, "Yes, Lord, I will pray in firm faith in you and in your great love."

It is a mistake to limit the word "faith" to the forgiveness of sins and our acceptance as children of God. Faith includes far more. We must have faith in all that God is willing to do for us. We must have faith each day according to our special needs. God is infinitely great and powerful, and Christ has so much grace for each new day, that our faith must daily reach out afresh according to the need of the day.

When you enter into the inner chamber, even before you begin to pray, ask yourself: Do I really believe that God is here with me, and that the Lord Jesus will help me to pray, and I may expect to spend it in communion with my God?

Jesus often taught his disciples how indispensable faith is to true prayer. He will teach us this lesson too. Remain in fellowship with him, and ask him to strengthen your faith in his almighty power. Christ says to you and to me, as he did to Martha, "Did I not tell you that if you would believe you would see the glory of God?" (Jn 11:40).

6 The Word of God
Man shall not live by bread alone, but by every word that proceeds from the mouth of God. (Mt 4:4)

The illustration that our Lord uses, in which the Word of God is compared to our daily bread, is most instructive.

Bread is indispensable to life. We all understand this. However strong a person may be, if he takes no nourishment, he will grow weak and eventually die. Even so with the Word of God. It contains a heavenly principle and works powerfully in those who believe.

Bread must be eaten. I may know all about bread. I may have bread and may give it to others. I may have bread in my house and on my table in great abundance, but if through illness I am unable to eat it, I will die. And so a mere knowledge of God's Word and even the preaching of it to others will not help me. It is not enough to merely think about God's word; I must take it into my heart and life. In love and obedience I must appropriate the words of God, and let them take full possession of my heart. Then they will indeed be words of life.

Bread must be eaten daily. And the same is true of God's Word. The psalmist says: "Blessed is the man [whose] delight is in the law of the Lord, and on his law he meditates day and night" (Ps 1:1-2). "Oh, how I love thy law! It is my meditation all the day" (Ps 119:97). To secure a strong and powerful spiritual life God's Word every day is indispensable.

When on earth the Lord Jesus learned, loved, and obeyed the word of the Father. And if you seek fellowship with him, you will find him in his Word. Christ will teach you to commune with the Father, through the Word, even as was his custom. You will learn, like him, to live solely for the glory of God and the fulfillment of his Word.

7 How to Read God's Word

Blessed is the man who walks not in the counsel of the wicked, . . . but his delight is in the law of the Lord, and on his law he meditates day and night. (Ps 1:1, 2)

Here are some simple rules for Bible reading:

Read God's Word with great reverence. Meditate a moment in silence on the thought that the words come from God himself. Bow in deep reverence. Be silent before God. Let him reveal his Word in your heart.

Read with careful attention. If you read the words carelessly, thinking that you can grasp their meaning with your human understanding, you will use the words superficially and not enter into their depths. When someone tries to explain anything wonderful or beautiful to us, we give our entire attention to understanding what is said. How much higher and deeper are God's thoughts than our thoughts!

"As the heaven is higher than the earth, so are my thoughts higher than your thoughts." We need to give our undivided attention to understand even the superficial meaning of the words. How much harder to grasp the spiritual meaning!

Read expecting the guidance of God's Spirit. Only God's Spirit can make the Word a living power in our hearts and lives. Read Psalm 119. Notice how earnestly David prays that God will teach him, and open his eyes, and give him understanding, and incline his heart to God's ways. As you read, remember that God's Word and God's Spirit are inseparable.

Read with the firm purpose of keeping the Word day and night in your heart and in your life. The whole heart and the whole life must come under the influence of the Word. David said, "Oh, how I love thy law! It is my meditation all the day." Even in the midst of his daily work, the believer can cherish God's Word in his heart and meditate on it. Read Psalm 119 again, until you accept God's Word with all your heart, and pray that God will teach you to understand it and to carry out its precepts in your life.

8 The Word and Prayer
Give me life, O Lord, according to thy word! (Ps 119:107)

Prayer and the Word of God are inseparable and should always go together in the quiet time of the inner chamber. In his Word God speaks to me; in prayer I speak to God. If there is to be true communion, both God and I must take part. If I simply pray, without using God's Word, I am apt to use my own words and thoughts. But what really gives prayer its power is that I take God's thoughts from his Word and present them before him. Then I am enabled to pray according to God's Word. How indispensable God's Word is for all true prayer!

When I pray, I must seek to know God rightly. It is through the Word that the Holy Spirit gives me right thoughts of him. The Word will also teach me how wretched and sinful I am. It reveals to me all the wonders that God will do for me and the strength he will give me to do his will. The Word teaches me how to pray—with strong desire, with a firm faith, and with constant perseverance. The Word teaches me not only what I am, but what I may become through God's grace. And above all, it reminds me each day that Christ is the great Intercessor, and allows me to pray in his Name.

Learn this great lesson: renew your strength each day in God's Word, and so pray according to his will.

Then we turn to the other side—prayer. We need prayer when we read God's Word—prayer to be taught by God to understand his Word, prayer that through the Holy Spirit I may rightly know and use God's Word, prayer that I may see in the Word that Christ is all in all and will be all in me.

Through the Word and prayer, I approach God in Christ and offer myself to God and his service. Strengthened by the Holy Spirit, with his love poured into my heart, I may daily walk in that love.

9 Obedience
Listen to my voice, and do all that I command you. I will be your God. (Jer 11:4)

God gave this command to Israel when he gave them the law. But Israel had no power to keep the law, so God gave them a "New Covenant" to enable his people to live a life of obedience. We read, "I will write [my law] upon their hearts" (Jer 31:33); "I will put the fear of me in their hearts, that they may not turn from me" (Jer 32:40); "I will cause you to walk in my statutes" (Ez 36:27). These wonderful promises gave the assurance that obedience would be their delight.

"If a man loves me, he will keep my word, and my Father will love him, and we will come to him and make our home with him" (Jn 14:21-23). And in John 15:10, "If you keep my commandments, you will abide in my love." These words are an inexhaustible treasure. Faith can firmly trust Christ to enable us to live such a life of love and obedience.

No father can train his children unless they are obedient.

No teacher can teach a child who continues to disobey him. No general can lead his soldiers to victory without prompt obedience. Pray God to imprint this lesson on your heart: the life of faith is a life of obedience. As Christ lived in obedience to the Father, so we too need obedience for a life in the love of God.

Unfortunately, we often think, "I cannot be obedient; it is quite impossible." Yes, impossible to you, but not to God. He has promised to cause you to walk in his statutes. Pray and meditate on these words, and the Holy Spirit will enlighten your eyes, so that you will have power to do God's will. Let your fellowship with the Father and with the Lord Jesus Christ have as its one aim and object—a life of quiet, determined, unquestioning obedience.

10 Confession of Sin
If we confess our sins, he is faithful and just, and will forgive our sins and cleanse us from all unrighteousness. (1 Jn 1:9)

Too often the confession of sin is superficial, and often it is quite neglected. Few Christians realize how necessary it is to be in earnest about the matter, and few feel that an honest confession of sin gives power to live the life of victory over sin. In fellowship with the Lord Jesus we need to confess with a sincere heart every sin that may hinder our Christian lives.

David says, "I acknowledged my sin to thee, and I did not hide my iniquity; I said, 'I will confess my transgressions to the Lord'; then thou didst forgive the guilt of my sin. . . . Thou art a hiding place for me . . . thou dost encompass me with deliverance" (Ps 32:5, 7). David speaks of a time when he was unwilling to confess his sin: "When I declared not my sin, my body wasted away." But when he had confessed his sin, a wonderful change came.

Confession means not only that I confess my sin with shame, but that I hand it over to God, trusting him to take it away. Such a confession implies that I am wholly unable to get rid of my guilt, but by an act of faith I depend on God to deliver me. This deliverance means that I know my sins are forgiven, and also that Christ undertakes to cleanse me from the sin and keep me from its power.

If you seek fellowship with Jesus, confess each sin in the confident assurance that there is deliverance. Let there be a mutual understanding between the Lord Jesus and yourself that you will confess each sin and obtain forgiveness. Then you will know your Lord as "Jesus who saves his people from their sin." Believe that there is great power in the confession of sin, for the burden of sin is borne by our Lord and Savior.

11 The First Love
But I have this against you, that you have abandoned the love you had at first. (Rv 2:4)

Revelation 2:2-3 mentions eight signs showing the zeal and activity of the church at Ephesus. But there was one bad sign, and the Lord said: "Repent and do the works you did at first. If not, I will come to you and remove your lampstand from its place, unless you repent" (vv. 4-5). And what was this bad sign? "You have abandoned the love you had at first."

We find the same lack in the Church of the present day. There is zeal for the truth, there is continuous and persevering labor, but that which the Lord values most is wanting, the tender, fervent love for himself.

This is significant: a church, a community, or a Christian may be exemplary in every good work and yet be missing the love for the Lord Jesus in the inner chamber. They may have no personal, daily fellowship with Christ, and consequently all the manifold activities with which people satisfy themselves are as nothing in the eyes of the Master.

This book speaks of the fellowship of love with Christ in the inner chamber. Everything depends on this. Christ came from heaven to love us with the love with which the Father loved him. He suffered and died to win our hearts for this love, and his love can be satisfied with nothing less than a deep, personal love on our part.

Christ considers this of the first importance. Let us do so too. Many ministers and missionaries and Christian workers confess with shame that in spite of all their zeal in the Lord's work, their prayer life is defective because they have left their first love. Write this down on a piece of paper and remember it continually: *The love of Jesus must be all.*

12 The Holy Spirit
He will glorify me, for he will take what is mine and declare it to you. (Jn 16:14)

Our Lord, in the last night that he was with his disciples, promised to send the Holy Spirit as a Comforter. Although his bodily presence was removed, they would realize his presence in them and with them in a wonderful way. The Holy Spirit, as God, would so reveal Christ in their hearts that they would experience his presence with them continually. The Spirit would glorify Christ and would reveal the glorified Christ in heavenly love and power.

How little do Christians understand and believe and experience this glorious truth. We would fail in our duty as ministers if, in a book like this or in our preaching, we encouraged Christians to love the Lord Jesus, without at the same time warning them that it is not a duty they can perform in their own strength. No, that is impossible; it is God, the Holy Spirit alone, who will pour his love into our hearts, and teach us to love him fervently. Through the Holy Spirit we may experience the love and abiding presence of the Lord Jesus all the day.

But remember that the Holy Spirit must have entire possession of us. He claims our whole heart and life. He will strengthen us with might in the inner man, so that we have fellowship with Christ, and keep his commandments, and abide in his love.

When once we have grasped this truth, we will experience our deep dependence on the Holy Spirit and will pray to the Father to send him in power into our hearts. The Spirit will teach us to love the Word, to meditate on it and to keep it. He will reveal the love of Christ to us, that we may love him fervently and with a pure heart. Then we shall begin to see that a life in the love of Christ in the midst of our daily life and distractions is a glorious possibility and a blessed reality.

13 Christ's Love for Us
As the Father has loved me, so have I loved you; abide in my love. (Jn 15:9)

In relationships between friends and among family members everything depends on love for each other. Of what value is abundance of riches if love is lacking between husband and wife, or parents and children? And in our Christian lives, of what value is all knowledge and zeal in God's work, without the knowledge and experience of Christ's love? (See 1 Cor 13:1-3.) The one thing needful in the inner chamber is to know by experience how much Christ loves you, and to learn how you may abide and continue in that love.

Think of what Christ says: "As the Father has loved me so have I loved you." What a divine, everlasting, wonderful love! It was the same love with which the Father had loved him and that he always bore in his heart, which he now gave into the hearts of his disciples. He yearns to have this everlasting love rest upon us and work within us, that we may abide in it day by day. Christ desires every disciple to live in the power of the same love of God that he himself experienced. Do you realize that in your fellowship with Christ in secret or in public, you are surrounded by and kept in this heavenly love? Let your desire reach out to this everlasting love. The Christ with whom you desire fellowship longs unspeakably to fill you with his love.

Read from time to time what God's Word says about the love of Christ. Meditate on the words, and let them sink into your heart. Sooner or later you will begin to realize this: The greatest happiness of my life is that I am beloved of the Lord Jesus. I may live in fellowship with him all the day long.

Let your heart continually say, "His love to me is unspeakable; he will keep me abiding in his love."

14 Our Love for Christ

Without having seen him you love him; though you do not now see him you believe in him and rejoice with unutterable and exalted joy. (1 Pt 1:8)

What a wonderful description of the Christian life! People who had never seen Christ, and yet truly loved him and believed in him, found that their hearts were filled with unspeakable joy. Such is the life of a Christian who really loves his Lord.

The chief attribute of the Father and of the Son is love for each other and for man. This should be the chief characteristic of the true Christian. The love of God and of Christ is poured into his heart and becomes a well of living water, flowing forth as love for the Lord Jesus.

This love is not merely a feeling. It is an active principle. It takes pleasure in doing the will of the Lord. It is joy to keep his commandments. The love of Christ for us was shown by his death on the cross; our love must be exhibited in unselfish, self-sacrificing lives. *In the Christian life love for Christ is everything!*

Great love will beget great faith—faith in his love for us, faith in the powerful revelations of his love in our hearts, faith that through his love he will work all his good pleasure in us.

The wings of faith and love will lift us up to heaven, and we will be filled with unspeakable joy. The joy of the Christian is an indispensable witness to the world of the power of Christ to change hearts and fill them with heavenly love and gladness.

Take time with him daily in the inner chamber and drink in his heavenly love. It will make your faith strong and your joy full. Love, joy, faith—these will be our life each day through the grace of our Lord Jesus.

15 Love for Our Brothers and Sisters in the Lord
A new commandment I give to you, that you love one another; even as I have loved you, that you also love one another. (Jn 13:34; see also Jn 15:12)

The Lord Jesus told his disciples that as the Father had loved him, so he loved them. And now, following his example, we must love one another with the same love. "By this all men will know that you are my disciples, if you have love for one another" (Jn 13:35). He had prayed, "That they may all be one; even as thou, Father, art in me, and I in thee, that they may also be in us, so that the world may believe that thou has sent me" (Jn 17:21). If we exhibit the love that was in God for Christ, and in Christ for us, the world will be obliged to confess that our Christianity is genuine and from above.

This is what actually happened. The Greeks and Romans, Jews and pagans, hated each other. Among all the nations of the world there was hardly a thought of love to each other. The very idea of self-sacrifice was a strange one. When people saw that Christians from different nations, under the powerful workings of the Holy Spirit, became one and loved one another, even to the point of self-sacrifice in time of plague or illness, they were amazed and said, "See how these people love one another!"

Among professing Christians there is a certain oneness of belief and feeling of brotherhood, but Christ's heavenly love is often lacking. We do not bear one another's burdens or love others heartily.

Pray that you may love your fellow-believers with the same love with which Christ loved you. If we abide in Christ's love and let that love fill our hearts, supernatural power will be given us to love all God's children from our hearts. As close as is the bond of love between the Father and the Son, between Christ and his followers, so close must the bond of love be between all God's children.

16 Love for Souls
Let him know that whoever brings back a sinner from the error of his way will save his soul from death. (Jas 5:20)

What a wonderful thought—that I may save a soul from everlasting death. How can this be? If I convert him from the error of his ways. This is the calling not only of the minister but of every Christian—to work for the salvation of sinners.

When Christ and his love took possession of our hearts, he gave us this love that we might bring others to him. In this way Christ's kingdom was extended. Everyone who had the love of Christ in his heart was constrained to tell others. This was the case in the early Christian church. After the day of Pentecost, people went out and told of the love of Christ, which they had themselves experienced. Pagan writers have told us that the rapid spread of Christianity in the first century was due to the fact that each convert, being filled with the love of Christ, tried to bring the good news to others.

What a change has come over the Church! Many Christians never try to win others to Christ. Their love is so weak and faint that they have no desire to help others. May the time soon come when Christians will feel constrained to tell of the love of Christ. In a revival in Korea a few years ago, the converts were filled with such a burning love for Christ that they felt bound to tell others of his love. It was even taken as a test of membership that each one should have brought another to the Lord before being admitted to the church.

Examine yourself, and pray that in fellowship with Christ you may think, not only of your own soul, but having received the gift of God's love you may pass it on to others. You will then know true happiness, the joy of bringing others to Christ.

Let us pray earnestly to be so filled with God's love that we may wholeheartedly surrender ourselves to win others for him.

17 The Spirit of Love

God's love has been poured into our hearts through the Holy Spirit which has been given to us. (Rom 5:5)
The fruit of the Spirit is love. (Gal 5:22)

The thought sometimes arises, as we consider Christ's love for us, our love for Christ, our love for our brothers and sisters, and our love for the souls around us, that the demand is too great, that it is unattainable. It seems impossible for a Christian to live this life of love and to show it to others. And because we consider it impossible, and because of our unbelief and lack of faith in God's promises, we make little progress in this spirit of love.

We need to continually remind ourselves that it is not by our own strength or even by serious thought that we can attain to the love of Christ. We must realize that the love of God is poured into our hearts and will be poured into them afresh every day by the Spirit of God. It is only as we are wholly surrendered to the leading of the Spirit that we will be able to live according to God's will. When the inner life of love is renewed from day to day we will feel compelled to work for souls.

Here is a prayer that you can offer: "I bow my knees before the Father . . . that he may grant you to be strengthened with might through his Spirit in the inner man, and that Christ may dwell in your hearts through faith; that you, being rooted and grounded in love, . . . may know the love of Christ which surpasses knowledge" (Eph 3:14, 16-17, 19). You may be rooted and grounded in this love that surpasses knowledge, but on one condition: you must be strengthened by the Spirit in the inner man, so that Christ may dwell in your heart. Then you will indeed be rooted and grounded in love.

Take this message from God's Word and let it influence your life. Unless you wait upon God daily to reveal his Spirit in your heart, you cannot live in this love. A life of prayer will make a life in the love of Christ and in the love of others a blessed reality in your experience.

Put your confidence each day in the Holy Spirit—the Spirit of love which God will give to those who ask in faith.

18 Persevering Prayer
They ought always to pray and not lose heart. (Lk 18:1)
Be constant in prayer. (Rom 12:12)
Pray constantly. (1 Thes 5:17)

One of the greatest drawbacks to the life of prayer is the fact that the answer may not come as speedily as we expect. We are discouraged and think: "Perhaps I am not praying right," and so we do not persevere in prayer. This was a lesson that our Lord taught often and urgently. If we consider the matter we can see that there may be a reason for the delay, and the waiting may actually be a blessing. Our desire must grow deeper and stronger, and we must ask with our whole heart. God puts us into the practicing school of persevering prayer, that our weak faith may be strengthened. There is a great blessing in the delayed answer to prayer.

Above all, God desires to draw us into closer fellowship with himself. When our prayers are not answered, we learn to realize that the fellowship and nearness and love of God are more to us than the answers of our petitions, and we continue in prayer. What a blessing Jacob received through the delay in the answer to his prayer! He saw God face to face, and as a prince he had power with God and prevailed.

Do not be impatient or discouraged if the answer does not come. "Be constant in prayer." "Pray constantly." You will find it an unspeakable blessing to do so. You will ask whether your prayer is really in accordance with the will of God and the Word of God. You will inquire if it is in the right spirit and in the name of Christ. Keep on praying. You will learn that the delay in the answer to prayer is one of the most precious means of grace that God can bestow on you. You will learn, too, that those who have persevered often and long before God, pleading his promises, are those who have had the greatest power with God in prayer.

19 The Prayer Meeting

All these with one accord devoted themselves to prayer. . . . And they were all filled with the Holy Spirit. (Acts 1:14; 2:4; see also Mt 18:19, 20)

Great is the value of a genuine prayer meeting. There God's children meet together, not as in church to listen to one speaker, but to lift up their hearts unitedly to God. By this means Christians are drawn closer to each other. Those who are weak are strengthened and encouraged by the testimony of the older and more experienced members, and even young Christians have the opportunity to tell of the joy of the Lord.

The prayer meeting may become a great power for good in a congregation and a spiritual help to both minister and members. By means of intercession God's blessing is poured out at home and abroad.

But there are also dangers to be considered. Many attend and are edified but never learn to pray themselves. Others go for the sake of social and religious fervor and have a form of godliness, but do not know the hidden life of prayer. Unless there is much and earnest prayer in the inner chamber, attendance at a prayer meeting may be a mere form. There should be hearty love and fellowship between the members. It is well to ask: What constitutes a living prayer meeting?

The leaders should realize how great the influence of such a meeting may be, with its roots nourished by the life of prayer in the inner chamber. Prayer should include God's people and his Church all over the world. And above all, as on the day of Pentecost, there must be waiting on God for the filling with the Holy Spirit.

This book aims at helping you in your spiritual life, but remember that you do not live for yourself alone. You are part of the body of Christ. Your intercession must include all Christians. As the roots of the tree hidden deep in the earth, and the branches spread out to heaven are one, so the hidden prayer life is inseparably bound up with united prayer.

20 Intercession
Pray at all times in the Spirit, . . . making supplication for all the saints. (Eph 6:18)

What an unspeakable blessing there is in intercession. That one should pray down heavenly gifts on himself is a wonder of grace, but that he should bring down blessings on others is indeed an inconceivable honor. Will God indeed make the pouring out of blessing on others dependent on our prayers? Yes, he makes us his remembrancers and fellow-workers. He has taken us into partnership in his work; if we fail in doing our part, others will suffer and his work will suffer.

God has appointed intercession as one of the means by which souls shall be saved, and saints and ministers of the gospel edified and built up in the faith. Even the ends of the earth will receive life and blessing through our prayers. Should we not expect God's children to strive joyfully and with all their powers, by means of intercession, to bring down blessing on the world?

Begin to use intercession as a means of grace for yourself and for others. Pray for your neighbors. Pray for souls with the definite desire that they may be won for Christ. Pray for your minister, for all ministers and missionaries. Pray for your country and people, for rulers and subjects. Pray for all men. If you surrender yourself to the guidance of the Holy Spirit and live a life wholly for God, you will realize that the time spent in prayer is an offering pleasing to God, bringing blessing to yourself and power into the lives of those for whom you pray.

Yes, "pray at all times in the Spirit, with all prayer and supplication. To that end keep alert with all perseverance, making supplication for all the saints." And in so doing you will learn the lesson that intercession is the chief means of winning souls and bringing glory to God.

21 Prayer and Fasting
He said to them, "Because of your little faith. . . . But this kind never comes out except by prayer and fasting." (Mt 17:20, 21)

Our Lord here teaches us that a life of faith requires both prayer and fasting. That is, prayer grasps the power of heaven, and fasting loosens the hold on earthly pleasure.

Jesus himself fasted to get strength to resist the devil. He taught his disciples that even as with prayer and almsgiving, fasting should be in secret, and the heavenly Father would reward openly. Abstinence from food, or temperance in taking it, strengthens the soul for communion with God.

Abstinence, temperance, and self-denial in temporal things helps the spiritual life. After having eaten a hearty meal, one does not feel much desire to pray. To willingly sacrifice our own pleasure or bodily enjoyment, and to subdue the lust of the flesh and the lust of the eyes, will help to set our minds more fully on heavenly things. The very exertion needed in overcoming the desires of the flesh will strengthen us to take hold of God in prayer.

Our dullness in prayer often comes from our fleshly desire of comfort and ease. "Those who are in Christ have crucified the flesh and its desires." Prayer is no easy work. It may easily become a mere form. For the real practice of prayer, for taking hold of God and having communion with him, it is necessary that all that pleases the flesh be sacrificed and given over to death.

It is worth any trouble to deny ourselves daily, in order to meet the Holy God and receive from him heavenly blessings.

22 The Spirit of Prayer
The Spirit intercedes for the saints. (Rom 8:27)

"Prayer is not our work, but God's work, that he works within us by his almighty power." We should expect that as we pray, the Holy Spirit will help us in our weakness and pray within us with "sighs too deep for words" (Rom 8:26).

What a thought! When I feel how defective my prayer is,

when I have no strength of my own, I may bow in silence before God in the confidence that his Holy Spirit will teach me to pray. The Spirit is the Spirit of prayer. It is not my work, but God's work in me. My very desire is a sign that God will hear me. When God would grant our requests, he first works the desire in our hearts, and the Spirit will perfect the work, even in our weakness. We see this in the story of Jacob. The same One who wrestled with him and seemed to withhold the blessing was in reality strengthening him to continue and to prevail in prayer. What a wonderful thought! Prayer is the work of the Triune God: the Father, who wakens the desire and will give us all we need; the Son, who through his intercession, teaches us to pray in his name; and the Holy Spirit, who in secret will strengthen our feeble desires.

We have spoken of the Spirit of truth who will glorify Christ in us, and of the Spirit of love, who will pour this love into our hearts. And now we have the Spirit of prayer, through whom our life may be one of continual prayer. Thank God. The Spirit has been given from heaven to dwell in our hearts and to teach us to pray.

Listen to the leading of the Spirit and obey his voice in all things. He will make you a man or a woman of prayer. You will then realize the glory of your calling as intercessor, asking great things of God for those around you, for the Church, and for the whole world.

23 Wholly for Christ
One has died for all . . . that those who live might live no longer for themselves but for him who for their sake died and was raised. (2 Cor 5:14, 15)

Here we have a threefold life described. First, the life of the Christian who lives according to his old nature: he lives for himself alone. The second, the life of a true Christian: he lives wholly for Christ. The third, the life of Christ in heaven: he lives wholly for us.

Many Christians need to be convinced of the folly of living only for themselves. At conversion they think more of their own salvation, and less of the glory of God and the right that Christ who has redeemed them with his precious blood has upon them. Many Christians just live for themselves, content with doing a little for the Master. Happy the believers who realize their high calling and the privilege and blessedness of consecrating their lives entirely to God's service.

The great hindrance to such a life is the unbelief which says it is impossible. But when the truth takes hold of us—Christ in heaven lives wholly for me and will impart his life to me, enabling me to live wholly for him—then we will be able to say joyfully, "Lord Jesus, from this moment let my prayer each day be 'Wholly for Christ, wholly for Christ.'"

Let nothing less than this be your earnest desire, your prayer, and your firm expectation: Christ has not only died for me, but lives in heaven to keep and sanctify me, his purchased possession. Ponder the wonderful thought that Christ will keep you as a member of his body, to work and live for him. Pray for grace to live wholly for God, in seeking souls and in serving his people. Take time from day to day to be so united to Christ in the inner man that you can say with all your heart: I live wholly for him, who gave himself wholly for me, and now lives in heaven wholly for me.

24 The Cross of Christ
I have been crucified with Christ. (Gal 2:20)

The cross of Christ is his greatest glory. "He humbled himself unto death . . . on a cross; *therefore* God has highly exalted him." The cross was the power that conquered Satan and sin.

The Christian shares with Christ in the cross. The crucified Christ lives in him through the Holy Spirit, and the spirit of the cross inspires him. He lives as one who has died with Christ. As he realizes the power of Christ's crucifixion, he lives as one who has died to the world and to sin, and the power becomes a reality in his life. It is as the Crucified One that Christ lives in me.

Our Lord said to his disciples, "Take up your cross and follow me." Did they understand this? They had seen men carrying a cross and knew what it meant—a painful death on the cross. And so all his life Christ bore his cross—the death sentence that he should die for the world. And each Christian must bear his or her cross, acknowledging that he is worthy of death, believing that he is crucified with Christ and that the Crucified One lives in him. "Our old man is crucified with Christ." "Those who belong to Christ have crucified the flesh with its passions and desires." When we have accepted this life of the cross, we will be able to say with Paul: "Far be it from me to glory except in the cross of our Lord Jesus Christ" (Gal 2:14).

This is a deep spiritual truth. Think and pray about it, and the Holy Spirit will teach you. Let the disposition of Christ on the cross, his humility, his sacrifice of all worldly honor, his self-denial, take possession of you. The power of his death will work in you, you will become like him in his death, and you will know him and the power of his resurrection. Take time, that Christ through his Spirit may reveal himself as the Crucified One.

25 The World
Do not love the world or the things in the world. If any one loves the world, love for the Father is not in him. (1 Jn 2:15)

John teaches us clearly what he means by "the world." He says, "For all that is in the world, the lust of the flesh and the lust of the eyes and the pride of life, is not of the Father but is of the world" (1 Jn 2:16).

"The world" is that disposition or power under which man has fallen through sin. And the god of this world, in order to deceive man, conceals himself under the form of what God has created. The world with its pleasures daily surrounds the Christian with temptations.

This was the case with Eve in the Garden of Eden. We find in Genesis 3 the three characteristics which John mentions: 1) The lust of the flesh—"The woman saw that the tree was good for food"; 2) The lust of the eyes—"It was a delight to the eyes"; 3) The pride of life—"It was to be desired to make one wise." And the world still comes to us offering desirable food and much to please the fleshly appetites; offering much that the eye desires, riches and beauty and luxury; and offering the pride of life, when a man imagines he knows and understands everything, and prides himself on it.

Is our life in the world not full of danger, with the allurements of the flesh—so much to occupy our eyes and our hearts, so much worldly wisdom and knowledge?

So John tells us, "Do not love the world." The Lord calls us, as he called his disciples of old, to leave all and follow him.

We live in a dangerous world. Cleave fast to the Lord Jesus. As he teaches you to shun the world and its attractions, your love will go out to him in loyal-hearted service. But remember, there must be daily fellowship with Jesus. His love alone can expel the love of the world. Take time to be alone with the Lord.

26 Put On Christ

For as many of you as were baptized into Christ have put on Christ. (Gal 3:27)
But put on the Lord Jesus Christ, and make no provision for the flesh, to gratify its desires. (Rom 13:14)

The word that is here translated "put on," is the same that is used in regard to putting on clothes. We have put on "the new man," and we have the new nature as a garment that is worn, by means of which all can see who we are. Paul says that the Christian who has confessed Christ at baptism has put on Christ. As a man may be recognized by the clothes he wears, so the Christian is known as one who has put on Christ, and exhibits him in his whole life and character.

And again Paul says, "Put on the Lord Jesus." Not just at conversion, but from day to day. As I put on my clothes each day and am seen in them, so the Christian must daily put on the Lord Jesus, so that he no longer lives after the flesh to fulfill its lusts, but shows forth the image of his Lord and the new man formed in his likeness.

Put on Christ. This work must be done each day in the inner chamber. I must put on the Lord, the heavenly Jesus.

As my garments cover me and protect me from wind and sun, even so Christ Jesus will be my beauty, my defence, and my joy. As I commune with him in prayer, he imparts himself to me and strengthens me to walk as one who is in him, and bound to him forever.

Take time to meditate on this truth. Just as your clothing is a necessity as you go out into the world, let it be equally indispensable for you to put on Jesus Christ, to abide in him and walk with him all day.

This cannot be done hastily and superficially. It takes time, quiet time in living fellowship with Jesus, to realize that you have put him on. Take the time and the trouble. Your reward will be great.

27 The Strength of the Christian
Finally, be strong in the Lord and in the strength of his might. (Eph 6:10)

The Apostle has reached the end of his epistle and begins his last division with the words, "Finally, be strong in the Lord."

The Christian needs strength. This we all know. The Christian has no strength of his own. This is also true. Where may strength be obtained? "Be strong *in the Lord* and in the strength of his might."

Paul spoke of this power in the earlier part of this epistle (Eph 1:18-20). He asked God to give them the Spirit that they might know "the immeasurable greatness of his power . . . according to the working of his great might which he accomplished in Christ when he raised him from the dead." This is the literal truth: the immeasurable greatness of his power, which raised Christ from the dead, works in *everyone* who believes. In me and in you. We hardly believe it, and still less do we experience it. That is why Paul prays, and we must pray with him, that God through his Spirit would teach us to believe in his almighty power. Pray with all your heart, "Father, grant me the Spirit of wisdom, that I may experience this power in my life."

In Ephesians 3:16, 17, Paul prays the Father to grant them, according to the riches of his glory, to be strengthened with might through his Spirit in the inner man, and that Christ might dwell in their hearts. And then: "Now to him who by the power at work within us is able to do far more abundantly than all that we ask or think, to him be glory in the church and Christ Jesus to all generations, for ever and ever" (vv. 20-21).

Read these two passages again, and pray for God's Spirit to enlighten you. Believe in the divine power working within you. Pray that the Holy Spirit may reveal it to you, and appropriate the promise that God will manifest his power in your heart, supplying all your needs.

Are you beginning to realize that time is needed, much time in fellowship with the Father and the Son, if you would experience the power of God within you?

28 The Whole Heart
With my whole heart I seek thee. (Ps 119:10)

Notice how often the psalmist speaks of the whole heart: "...who seek him with their whole heart" (v. 2); "Observe it with my whole heart" (v. 34); "With my whole heart I keep thy precepts" (v. 69); "With my whole heart I cry" (v. 145). In seeking God, in observing his law, in crying for his help—each time it is with the whole heart.

When we want to succeed in worldly affairs, we put our whole heart into it. And is this not much more necessary in the service of a holy God? Is he not worthy? Does not his great holiness and the natural aversion of our hearts from God demand it? The whole heart is needed in the service of God when we worship him in secret.

And yet how little most Christians think of this. They do not remember how necessary it is—in prayer, in reading God's Word, in striving to do his will—to say continually: "With my *whole heart* I seek thee." Yes, when we pray, and when we try to understand God's word, and to obey his commands let us say: I desire to seek God, to serve him, and to please him with my whole heart.

"With my whole heart I seek thee." Take this word into your heart. Think about it. Pray about it. Speak it out before God until you really mean what you say and are assured that

God will hear your prayer. Say it each morning as you approach God in prayer. I seek thee with my whole heart. You will by degrees feel the need of waiting in holy stillness upon God, that he may take possession of your whole heart, and you will learn to love him with your whole heart and with all your strength.

29 In Christ
He is the source of your life in Christ Jesus, whom God made our wisdom, our righteousness and sanctification and redemption. (1 Cor 1:30)

The expression "in Christ" is often used in the epistles. The Christian cannot read God's Word correctly, nor experience its full power in his life, until he prayerfully and believingly accepts this truth: I am in Christ Jesus.

The Lord Jesus, on the last night with his disciples, used these words more than once. "In that day" (when the Spirit had been poured out), "You will know that I am in my Father, and you in me" (Jn 14:20). And then follows "Abide in me . . . he who abides in me . . . bears much fruit" (Jn 15:4-5). "If you abide in me, . . . ask whatever you will, and it shall be done for you" (Jn 15:7). But the Christian cannot appropriate these promises unless he first prayerfully accepts the words "in Christ."

Paul expresses the same thought in Romans: "We are buried with Christ"; "You must consider yourselves dead to sin and alive to God in Christ Jesus" (5:11); "There is . . . no condemnation for those who are in Christ Jesus" (8:1). And in Ephesians: God "has blessed us in Christ with every spiritual blessing" (1:3); "He chose us in him" (1:4); "In him we have redemption" (1:7). And in Colossians: we are "perfect in Christ Jesus"; "Walk in him"; "You have come to fullness of life in him."

Let our faith take hold of the words: "It is God who establisheth us in Christ." "Of God I am in Christ Jesus." The Holy Spirit will make it our experience. Pray earnestly and follow the leading of the Spirit. The word will take root in your heart, and you will realize something of its heavenly power. But remember that abiding in Christ is a matter of the heart. It must be cultivated in a spirit of love. Only as we take time from day to day in fellowship with Christ will the abiding in Christ become a blessed reality and the inner man will be renewed from day to day.

30 Christ in Me
Do you not realize that Jesus Christ is in you?
(2 Cor 13:5)

The Apostle would have each Christian live in the full assurance: Christ is in me. What a difference it would make in our lives if we could take time every morning to be filled with the thought: Christ is in me. As assuredly as I am in Christ, Christ is also in me.

On the last night Christ put it clearly to his disciples, that the Spirit would teach them: "In that day you will know that I am in my Father, and you in me, and I in you" (Jn 14:20). First of all, you in me. Through the power of God all we who believe were crucified with Christ and raised again with him. As a result, Christ is in us. But this knowledge does not come easily. Through faith in God's Word the Christian accepts it, and the Holy Spirit will lead us into all truth. Take time this very day to realize and appropriate this blessing in prayer.

How clearly Paul expresses the thought in the prayer of Ephesians 3:16: "That according to the riches of his glory he may grant you to be strengthened with might through his Spirit in the inner man." Notice that it is not the ordinary gift of grace, but a special revelation of the riches of his love and power. "That he grant you to be strengthened with might through his Spirit in the inner man," so that "*Christ may dwell in your hearts by faith.*" Have you grasped it? The Christian may really have the experience of being filled with the fullness of God.

Paul said, "I bow my knees before the Father." That is the only way to obtain the blessing. Take time in the inner chamber to realize: Christ dwells in me. Too little have I experienced this in the past, but I will cry to God and wait upon him to perfect his work in me. Even in the midst of my daily work, I must look upon my heart as the dwelling place of the Son of God, and say: "I have been crucified with Christ; it is no longer I who live, but Christ who lives in me" (Gal 2:20). Only in this way will Christ's words, "Abide in me, and I in you," become my daily experience.

31 Christ Is All
Christ is all, and in all. (Col 3:11)

In the eternal counsel of God, in the redemption on the cross, as King on the throne in heaven and on earth—Christ is all!

Have you perhaps thought in reading these pages that the full salvation here described is not meant for you? You feel too weak, too unworthy, too untrustworthy. Then believe that if you will only accept the Lord Jesus in childlike faith, you have a leader and a guide who will supply all your need. Believe with your whole heart in the word of our Savior, "Lo, I am with you always" (Mt 28:20), and you will experience his presence each day. However cold and dull your feelings may be, however sinful you are, meet the Lord Jesus in secret and he will reveal himself to you. Tell him how miserable you are, and then trust him to help and sustain you. Wait before him until by faith you can rejoice in him. Read this book over again, and read it with this thought: Christ is all. I have failed to remember this, but each day as I go to secret prayer let this thought be with me: Christ is all. Let me take it as my motto—to teach me to pray, to strengthen my faith, to assure me of his love and my access to the Father, to make me strong for the work of the day: Christ is all. Yes, Christ, my Christ, is all I need. It will teach me to abide in his love. It will give me the assurance that he dwells in my heart, that I may know the love that passes knowledge. God be praised to all eternity: Christ, my Christ, is my all in all!

Month Two

1 Intercession
Pray for one another. (Jas 5:16)

What a mystery of glory there is in prayer! On the one hand we see God, in his holiness and love and power, waiting, longing to bless man; and on the other, sinful man, a worm of the dust, bringing down from God by prayer the very life and love of heaven to dwell in his heart.

But how much greater the glory of intercession!—when a man makes bold to say to God what he desires for others, and seeks to bring down on one soul, or it may be on hundreds and thousands, the power of the eternal life with all its blessings.

Intercession! Would one not say that this is the very holiest exercise of our boldness as God's children, the highest privilege and enjoyment connected with our communion with God—the power of being used by God as instruments for his great work of making men his habitation and showing forth his glory?

One would think that the Church would count this one of the chief means of grace and seek above everything to cultivate in God's children the power of an unceasing prayerfulness on behalf of the perishing world.

Would we not expect that believers, who have to some extent been brought into the secret, would feel what strength there is in unity and what assurance there is that

God will certainly avenge his own elect who cry day and night to him? It is when Christians cease from looking for help in external union and aim at all being bound together to the throne of God, by an unceasing devotion to Jesus Christ and an unceasing continuance in supplication for the power of God's Spirit, that the Church will put on her beautiful garments, and put on her strength too, and overcome the world.

Our gracious Father, hear our prayer and teach your Church, and teach each of us, what is the glory, what the blessing, what the all-prevailing power of intercession. Give us, we pray, the vision of what intercession means to you, as essential for carrying out your purpose, and what it means to ourselves as the exercise of our royal priesthood, and what it will mean to your Church and to perishing men, in bringing down the Spirit in power. Amen.

2 The Opening of the Eyes

Then Elisha prayed, and said, "O Lord, I pray thee, open his eyes that he may see." ... Elisha said, "O Lord, open the eyes of these men, that they may see." (2 Kgs 6:17, 20)

How wonderfully the prayer of Elisha for his servant was answered! The young man saw the mountain full of chariots of fire and horsemen about Elisha. The heavenly host had been sent by God to protect his servant.

A second time Elisha prayed. The Syrian army had been struck blind and so led into Samaria. There Elisha prayed for the opening of their eyes, and they found themselves hopeless prisoners in the hand of the enemy.

We wish to use these prayers in the spiritual sphere, first of all, to ask that our eyes may see the wonderful provision that God has made for his Church in the baptism with the Holy Spirit and with fire. All the powers of the heavenly world are at our disposal in the service of the heavenly kingdom. How little the children of God live in the faith of that heavenly vision—the power of the Holy Spirit, on them, with them, and in them, for their own spiritual life, and as their strength joyfully to witness for their Lord and his work!

But we need that second prayer too, that God may open the eyes of those of his children who do not as yet see the power which the world and sin have upon his people. They are as yet unconscious of the feebleness that marks the Church, making it impotent to do the work of winning souls for Christ and building up believers for a life of holiness and fruitfulness. Let us pray especially that God may open all eyes to see the great and fundamental need of the Church in intercession to bring down his blessing, that the power of the Spirit may be known unceasingly in its divine efficacy and blessing.

Father in heaven, you who are so unspeakably willing to give us the Holy Spirit in power, hear our humble prayer. Open our eyes, we pray, that we may realize fully the low estate of your Church and people, and as fully what treasures of grace and power you are willing to bestow in answer to the fervent prayer of a united Church. Amen.

3 Man's Place in God's Plan
The heavens are the Lord's heavens, but the earth he has given to the sons of men. (Ps 115:16)

God created heaven as a dwelling for himself—perfect, glorious, and most holy. The earth he gave to man as his dwelling—everything very good, but only as a beginning, needing to be kept and cultivated. The work God had done, man was to continue and perfect. Think of the iron and the coal hidden away in the earth, of the steam hidden away in the water. It was left to man to discover and to use all this, as we see in the network of railways that span the world and the steamers that cover the ocean. God had created all to be thus used. He made the discovery and the use dependent on the wisdom and diligence of man. What the earth is today, with its cities and habitations, with its cornfields and orchards, it owes to man. The work God had begun and prepared was to be carried out by man in fulfillment of God's purpose. So nature teaches us the wonderful partnership to which God calls man for the carrying out of the work of creation to its destined end.

This law holds equally good in the kingdom of grace. In this great redemption God has revealed the power of the heavenly life and the spiritual blessings of which heaven is full. *But he has entrusted to his people the work of making these blessings known and making men partakers of them.*

What diligence the children of this world show in seeking the treasures that God has hidden in the earth for their use! Shall not the children of God be equally faithful in seeking for the treasures hidden in heaven, to bring them down in blessing on the world? It is by the unceasing intercession of God's people that his kingdom will come and his will be done on earth as it is in heaven.

Lord, how wonderful is the place you hast given man in trusting him to continue the work you have begun. Open our hearts for the great thought that, through the preaching of the gospel and the work of intercession, your people are to work out your purpose. Lord, open our eyes. Amen.

4 Intercession in the Plan of Redemption
O thou who hearest prayer! To thee shall all flesh come. (Ps 65:2)

When God gave the world into the power of man, made in his own image, who should rule over it as a viceroy under him, it was his plan that Adam should do nothing but with God and through God, and God himself would do all his work in the world through Adam. Adam was indeed to be the owner, master, and ruler of the earth. When sin entered the world, Adam's power was proved to be a terrible reality, for through him the earth, with the whole race of man, was brought under the curse of sin.

God's object in redemption was to restore man to the place from which he had fallen. God chose his servants of old, who, through the power of intercession, could ask what they would and it would be given them. When Christ became man, it was so that, as man, both on earth and in heaven, he might intercede for man. And before he left the world, he imparted this right of intercession to his disciples in the seven-fold promise of the Farewell Discourse (Jn 15-17), that whatever they asked he would do for them. God's intense longing to bless seems in some sense to be graciously limited by his dependence on the intercession that rises from the earth. He seeks to rouse the spirit of intercession, that he may be able to bestow his blessing on mankind. God regards intercession as the highest expression of his people's readiness to receive and to yield themselves wholly to the working of his almighty power.

Christians need to realize this as their true nobility and their only power with God—the right to claim and expect that God will hear prayer. It is only as God's children begin to see what intercession means in regard to God's kingdom, that they will realize how solemn their responsibility is.

Each individual believer will be led to see that God waits for him to take his part. He will feel in very truth that the highest, the most blessed, the mightiest of all human instrumentalities for the fulfillment of the petition, "as in heaven, so on earth," is the intercession that rises day and night, pleading with God for the power of heaven to be sent down into the hearts of men. Oh that God might burn into our hearts this one thought: Intercession in its power is according to his will and is most certainly effectual!

5 God Seeks Intercessors
He saw that there was no man, and wondered that there was no one to intervene. (Is 59:16)

From of old God had among his people intercessors to whose voice he had listened and given deliverance. Here we read of a time of trouble when he sought for an intercessor, but in vain. And he wondered! Think of what that means— the amazement of God that there should be none who loved the people enough, or who had sufficient faith in his power to deliver, to intercede on their behalf. If there had been an intercessor he would have given deliverance; without an intercessor his judgments came down (see Is 64:7; Ez 22:30, 31).

Of what infinite importance is the place the intercessor holds in the kingdom of God! Is it not indeed a matter of wonder that God should give men such power, and yet that there are so few who know what it is to take hold of his strength and pray down his blessing on the world?

When God had in his Son wrought out the new creation, and Christ had taken his place on the throne, the work of the extension of his kingdom was given into the hands of men. Christ ever lives to pray; prayer is the highest exercise of his royal prerogative as Priest-King upon the throne. All that Christ was to do in heaven was to be in fellowship with his people on earth. In his divine condescension God has willed that the working of his Spirit shall follow the prayer of his people. He waits for their intercession, showing the preparation of heart—where and how much of his Spirit they are ready to receive.

God rules the world and his Church through the prayers of his people. "That God should have made the extension of his kingdom to such a large extent dependent on the faithfulness of his people in prayer is a stupendous mystery and yet an absolute certainty." God calls for intercessors. In his grace he has made his work dependent on them; he waits for them.

Father, open our eyes to see that you invite your children to have a part in the extension of your kingdom by their faithfulness in prayer and intercession. Give us such an insight into the glory of this holy calling, that with our whole heart we may yield ourselves to its service. Amen.

6 Christ As Intercessor
Consequently he is able for all time to save those who draw near to God through him, since he always lives to make intercession for them. (Heb 7:25)

When God had said in Isaiah that he wondered that there was no intercessor, there followed the words: "Then his own arm brought him victory. . . . He will come to Zion as Redeemer" (Is 59:16, 20). God himself would provide the true intercessor, in Christ his Son, of whom it had already been said, "He bore the sin of many, and made intercession for the transgressors" (Is 53:12).

In his life on earth Christ began his work as Intercessor. Think of the high-priestly prayer on behalf of his disciples and of all who should through them believe in his name. Think of his words to Peter, "I have prayed for you that your faith may not fail"—a proof of how intensely personal his intercession is. And on the cross he spoke as intercessor: "Father, forgive them."

Now that he is seated at God's right hand, he continues, as our great High Priest, the work of intercession without ceasing, but with this difference: he gives his people power to take part in it. Seven times in his Farewell Discourse he assured them that what they asked he would do. The power of heaven was to be at their disposal. The grace and power of God waited for man's bidding. Through the leading of the Holy Spirit they would know what the will of God was. They would learn in faith to pray in his name. He would present their petition to the Father, and through his and their united intercession the Church would be clothed with the power of the Spirit.

Christ, our Redeemer, what wonderful grace that you call us to share in your intercession! Arouse in your redeemed people a consciousness of the glory of this calling, and of all the rich blessing which your Church in its impotence can, through its intercession in your name, bring down upon this earth. May your Holy Spirit work in your people a deep conviction of the sin of restraining prayer, of the sloth and unbelief and selfishness that is the cause of it, and of your loving desire to pour out the Spirit of prayer in answer to their petitions. Amen.

7 The Intercessors God Seeks

Upon your walls, O Jerusalem, I have set watchmen; all the day and all the night they shall never be silent. You who put the Lord in remembrance, take no rest, and give him no rest. (Is 62:6, 7)

Watchmen are ordinarily placed on the walls of a city to notify the rulers of coming danger. God appoints watchmen not only to warn men—often they will not hear—but also to summon him to come to their aid whenever need or enemy may be threatening. The great mark of the intercessors is to be that they are not to hold their peace day or night, to take no rest and to give God no rest, until the deliverance comes. In faith they may count upon the assurance that God will answer their prayer.

It is of this that our Lord Jesus said: "Shall not God avenge his own elect, who cry to him day and night?" From every land the voice is heard that the Church of Christ, under the influence of the power of the world and the earthly-mindedness it brings, is losing its influence over its members. There is little proof of God's presence in the conversion of sinners or the holiness of his people. With the great majority of Christians there is an utter neglect of Christ's call to take a part in the extension of his kingdom. The power of the Holy Spirit is but little experienced.

Amid all the discussions as to how to interest young and old in the study of God's Word, or to awaken love for the services of his house, one hears little of the indispensable necessity of the power of the Holy Spirit in the ministry and the membership of the Church. One sees but little sign of the conviction and confession that it is owing to the lack of prayer that the workings of the Spirit are so feeble, and that only by united fervent prayer a change can be brought about. If ever there was a time when God's elect should cry day and night to him, it is now. Will you not offer yourself to God for this work of intercession and learn to count it the highest privilege of your life to be a channel through whose prayers God's blessing can be brought down to earth?

Father, hear us and raise up intercessors such as you would have. Give us men and women to act as your remembrancers, taking no rest and giving you no rest, until your Church again be a praise in the earth. Father, let your Spirit teach us how to pray. Amen.

8 The School of Intercession

In the days of his flesh, Jesus offered up prayers and supplications, with loud cries and tears, to him who was able to save him from death, and he was heard for his godly fear. (Heb 5:7)

Christ, as Head, is Intercessor in heaven; we, as the members of his body, are partners with him on earth. Let no one imagine that it cost Christ nothing to become an intercessor. He could not without this be our example. What do we read of him? "When he makes himself an offering for sin, he shall see his offspring, . . . he shall see the fruit of the travail of his soul. . . . I will divide him a portion with the great, . . . because he poured out his soul to death" (Is 53:10-12). Notice the expression in regard to the pouring out of his soul.

The pouring out of the soul—that is the divine meaning of intercession. Nothing less than this was needed if his sacrifice and prayer were to have power with God. This giving of himself over to live and die that he might save the perishing was a revelation of the Spirit that has power to prevail with God.

If we as helpers and fellow-laborers with the Lord Jesus are to share his power of intercession, there will need to be with us too the travail of soul that there was with him, the giving up of our life and its pleasures for the one supreme work of interceding for others. Intercession must not be a passing interest; it must become an ever-growing object of intense desire, for which we long and live. It is the life of consecration and self-sacrifice that will indeed give power for intercession (Acts 15:26; 20:24; Phil 2:17; Rv 12:11).

The longer we study this truth and think of what it means to exercise this power for the glory of God and the salvation of men, the deeper will become our conviction that it is worth giving up everything to take part with Christ in his work of intercession.

Lord Jesus, be pleased to teach us how to unite with you in calling upon God for the souls you have bought. Let your love fill us and all your saints, that we may learn to plead for the power of your Holy Spirit to be made known. Amen.

9 The Name of Jesus, the Power of Intercession
Hitherto you have asked nothing in my name; ask, and you will receive, that your joy may be full. (Jn 16:24, 26)

During Christ's life upon earth, the disciples had known but little of the power of prayer. In Gethsemane, Peter and the others had utterly failed. They had no conception of what it was to ask in the name of Jesus and to receive. The Lord promised them that in the day which was coming they would be able to pray with such a power in his name, that they might ask what they would and it should be given to them.

"Hitherto you have asked nothing in my name; ask, and you will receive." These two conditions are still found in the Church. The great majority of Christians lack a knowledge of their oneness with Christ Jesus and of the Holy Spirit as the Spirit of prayer, and they do not even attempt to claim the wonderful promises Christ here gives. But where God's children know what it is to abide in Christ and in vital union with him, and to yield to the Holy Spirit's teaching, they begin to learn that their intercession has great power and that God will give the power of his Spirit in answer to their prayer.

It is faith in the power of Jesus' name and in our right to use it, that will give us the courage to follow where God invites us, to the holy office of intercessors. When our Lord Jesus, in his Farewell Discourse, gave his unlimited prayer promise, he sent the disciples out into the world with this consciousness: "He who sits upon the throne, and who lives in my heart, has promised that what I ask in his name I shall receive. He will do it."

If only Christians knew what it is to yield themselves wholly and absolutely to Jesus Christ and his service, they would see that intense and unceasing prayerfulness is the essential mark of the healthy spiritual life, and that the power of all-prevailing intercession will indeed be the portion of those who live only in and for their Lord!

Christ our Savior, give us the grace of the Holy Spirit, to so much live in you, and with you, and for you, that we may boldly look to you for the assurance that our prayers are heard. Amen.

10 Prayer, the Work of the Spirit
God has sent the Spirit of his Son into our hearts, crying, "Abba! Father!" (Gal 4:6)

We know what "Abba, Father" meant in the mouth of Christ in Gethsemane. It was the entire surrender of himself to death, that the holy will of God's love in redemption of sinners might be accomplished. In his prayer he was ready for any sacrifice, even to the yielding of his life. In that prayer we have revealed to us the heart of him whose place is at the right hand of God, with the wonderful power of intercession that he exercises there and the power to pour down the Holy Spirit.

It is to breathe the very Spirit of his Son into our hearts that the Holy Spirit has been bestowed by the Father. The Lord wants us to yield ourselves as wholly to God as he did—to pray, like him, that God's will of love should be done on earth at any cost. As God's love is revealed in his desire for the salvation of souls, so also the desire of Jesus was made plain when he gave himself for them. And he now asks of his people that that same love should fill them too, so that they give themselves wholly to the work of intercession and, at any cost, pray down God's love upon the perishing.

And lest anyone should think that this is too high and beyond our reach, the Holy Spirit of Jesus is actually given into our hearts that we may pray in his likeness, in his name, in his power. It is the man who yields himself wholly to the leading of the Holy Spirit who will feel urged, by the compulsion of a divine love, to the undivided surrender to a life of continual intercession, because he knows that it is God who is working in him.

We can now understand how Christ could give such unlimited promises of answer to prayer to his disciples; they were first going to be filled with the Holy Spirit. We now understand how God can give such a high place to intercession in the fulfillment of his purpose of redemption; it is the Holy Spirit who breathes God's own desire into us and enables us to intercede for souls.

Abba, Father! Grant that by your Holy Spirit there may be maintained in us the unceasing intercession of love for the souls for whom Christ died. Give to your children the vision of the blessing and the power which come to those who yield themselves to this high calling. Amen.

11 Christ, Our Example in Intercession

He shall divide the spoil with the strong, because . . . he bore the sin of many, and made intercession for the transgressors. (Is 53:12)

"He made intercession for the transgressors." What did that mean to him? Think of what it cost him to pray that prayer effectually. He had to pour out his soul as an offering for sin and cry in Gethsemane, "Father, your holy will of love be done."

Consider what moved him to sacrifice himself to the very uttermost! It was his love for the Father—that his holiness might be manifest—and love for souls—that they might be partakers of his holiness.

Think of the reward he won! As Conqueror of every enemy, he is seated at the right hand of God, with the power of unlimited and assured intercession. And he would see his seed, a generation of those of the same mind with himself, whom he could train to a share in his great work of intercession.

And what does this mean for us, when we pray for the transgressors? That we, too, yield ourselves wholly to the glory of the holiness and the love of the Father, that we too say: your will be done, cost what it may; that we too sacrifice ourselves, even to pouring out our soul unto death.

Jesus has indeed taken us up into a partnership with himself, in carrying out the great work of intercession. He in heaven and we on earth must have one mind, one aim in life—that we should, from love for the Father and for the lost, consecrate our lives to intercession for God's blessing. The burning desire of Father and Son for the salvation of souls must be the burning desire of our heart too.

What an honor! What a power for us to do the work, because he lives and by his Spirit pours forth his love into our hearts!

Everlasting God of love, open our eyes to the vision of the glory of your Son, as he ever lives to pray. And open our eyes to the glory of that grace which enables us in his likeness also to live that we may pray for the transgressors. Amen.

12 God's Will and Ours
Thy will be done. (Mt 26:42)

It is the high prerogative of God that everything in heaven and earth is to be done according to his will and as the fulfillment of his desires. When he made man in his image it was, above all, that his desires were to be in perfect accord with the desires of God. This is the high honor of being in the likeness of God—that we are to feel and desire just as God. In human flesh man was to be the embodiment and fulfillment of God's desires.

When God created man with the power of willing and choosing what he should be, he limited himself in the exercise of his will. And when man had fallen and yielded himself to the will of God's enemy, God in his infinite love set about the great work of winning man back to make the desires of God his own. As in God, so in man, desire is the great moving power. And just as man had yielded himself to a life of desire after the things of the earth and the flesh, God had to redeem him and educate him into a life of harmony with himself. His one aim was that man's desire should be in perfect accord with his own.

The great step in this direction was when the Son of the Father came into this world, to reproduce the divine desires in his human nature and in his prayer to yield himself up to the perfect fulfillment of all that God wished and willed. The Son, as Man, said in agony and blood, "Your will be done" and surrendered even to the point of being forsaken by God, that the power that had deceived man might be conquered and deliverance procured. It was in the wonderful and complete harmony between the Father and the Son when the Son said, "Your will of love be done," that the great redemption was accomplished.

And this is now the great work of appropriating that redemption. Believers have to say, first of all for themselves and then in lives devoted to intercession for others; "Your will be done in heaven as on earth." As we plead for the Church—its ministers and its missionaries, its strong Christians or its young converts, for the unsaved, whether nominally Christian or not at all—we have the privilege of knowing that we are pleading for what God wills and that through our prayers his will is to be done on earth as in heaven.

13 The Blessedness of a Life of Intercession
You who put the Lord in remembrance, take no rest, and give him no rest until he establishes Jerusalem and makes it a praise in the earth. (Is 62:6, 7)

What an unspeakable grace to be allowed to deal with God in intercession for the supply of the need of others!

What a blessing, in close union with Christ, to take part in his great work as Intercessor and to mingle my prayers with his! What an honor to have power with God in heaven over souls and to obtain for them what they do not know or think!

What a privilege, as a steward of the grace of God, to bring to him the state of the Church or of individual souls, of the ministers of the Word or his missionaries, and plead on their behalf until he entrusts me with the answer!

What a blessing, in union with other children of God, to strive together in prayer until the victory is gained over difficulties here on earth and over the powers of darkness in high places!

It is indeed worth living for, to know that God will use me as an intercessor, to receive and dispense here on earth his heavenly blessing and above all the power of his Holy Spirit.

This is indeed the life of heaven, the life of the Lord Jesus himself, in his self-denying love, possessing me and urging me to yield myself wholly to bear the burden of souls before him and to plead that they may live.

Too long have we thought of prayer simply as a means for the supplying of our need in life and service. May God help us to see what a place intercession takes in his divine counsel and in his work for the kingdom. May our hearts indeed feel that there is no honor or pleasure on earth at all equal to the unspeakable privilege of waiting upon God of bringing down from heaven and opening the way on earth for the blessing he delights to give!

Father, let your life indeed flow down to this earth and fill the hearts of your children! As Jesus pours out his love in his unceasing intercession in heaven, let it be so with us upon earth, a life of overflowing love and never ending intercession. Amen.

14 The Place of Prayer
All these with one accord devoted themselves to prayer. (Acts 1:14)

The last words which Christ spoke before he left the world give us the four great marks of his Church: "Wait for the promise of the Father"; "Ye shall receive power when the Holy Spirit has come upon you"; "You shall be my witnesses"; "In Jerusalem and unto the end of the earth."

United and unceasing prayer, the power of the Holy Spirit, living witnesses to the living Christ, from Jerusalem to the end of the earth—such are the marks of the true gospel, the true ministry, the true Church of the New Testament.

A Church of united and unceasing prayerfulness, a ministry filled with the Holy Spirit, the members living witnesses to a living Christ, with a message to every creature on earth—such was the Church that Christ founded, and such was the Church that went out to conquer the world.

When Christ ascended to heaven, the disciples knew at once what their work was to be: continuing with one accord in prayer and supplication. They were to be bound together, by the love and Spirit of Christ, into one body. This gave them their wonderful power in heaven with God and upon earth with men.

Their own duty was to wait in united and unceasing prayer for the power of the Holy Spirit, as the enduement from on high for their witness to Christ to the ends of the earth. A praying Church, a Spirit-filled Church, a witnessing Church, with all the world as its sphere and aim—such is the Church of Jesus Christ.

As long as it maintained this character, it had power to

conquer. But as it has come under the influence of the world, how much it has lost of its heavenly, supernatural beauty and strength! How unfaithful in prayer, how feeble the workings of the Spirit, how formal its witness to Christ, and how unfaithful to its worldwide mission!

Lord Jesus, have mercy upon your Church and give it the Spirit of prayer and supplication as of old, that your Church may prove what power from you rests upon it and its testimony for you to win the world to your feet. Amen.

15 Paul as an Intercessor
For this reason I bow my knees before the Father, . . . that according to the riches of his glory he may grant you to be strengthened with might through his Spirit in the inner man. (Eph 3:14, 16)

We think of Paul as the great missionary, the great preacher, the great writer, the great apostle "in labors more abundant." We do not sufficiently think of him as an intercessor who sought and obtained by his supplication the power that rested upon all his other activities and brought down the blessing that rested on the churches that he served.

We see above what he wrote to the Ephesians. Consider what he said to the Thessalonians: "Praying earnestly night and day that we may . . . supply what is lacking in your faith . . . so that he may establish your hearts unblamable in holiness" (1 Thes 3:10, 13). To the Romans: "Without ceasing I mention you always in my prayers" (1:9). To the Philippians: "Always in every prayer of mine for you all making my prayer with joy" (1:4). And to the Colossians: "We have not ceased to pray for you. . . . I want you to know how greatly I strive for you" (1:9; 2:1).

Day and night he interceded for them, that the light and the power of the Holy Spirit might be in them; and as earnestly as he believed in the power of his intercession for them, he also believed in the blessing that theirs would bring upon him. "I appeal to you, brethren, . . . to strive together with me in your prayers to God on my behalf"

(Rom 15:30). "He will deliver us. . . . You also must help us by prayer" (2 Cor 1:10, 11). "Making supplication . . . also for me, that utterance may be given me in opening my mouth boldly" (Eph 6:18, 19; see also Col 4:3; 2 Thes 3:1). "Through your prayers . . . this will turn out for my deliverance" (Phil 1:19).

The whole relationship between pastor and people depends on the united continual prayerfulness. Their whole relationship is a heavenly one, spiritual and divine, and can only be maintained by unceasing prayer. It is when ministers and people awaken to the consciousness that the power and blessing of the Holy Spirit is waiting for their united and unceasing prayer, that the Church will begin to know something of what pentecostal apostolic Christianity is.

Father, graciously restore again to your Church the spirit of supplication and intercession. Amen.

16 Intercession for Laborers
The harvest is plentiful, but the laborers are few; pray therefore the Lord of the harvest to send out laborers into his harvest. (Mt 9:37, 38)

The disciples understood very little of what these words meant. Christ gave them as a seed-thought, to be lodged in their hearts for later use. At Pentecost, as they saw how many of the new converts were ready in the power of the Spirit to testify to Christ, they must have felt how the ten days of continuous united prayer had brought this blessing too, as the fruit of the Spirit's power—laborers in the harvest.

Christ meant to teach us that, however large the field may be and however few the laborers, prayer is the best, the sure, the only means for supplying the need.

What we need to understand is that it is not only in time of need that the prayer must be sent up, but that the whole work is to be carried on in the spirit of prayer, so that the prayer for laborers will be in perfect harmony with the whole of our life and effort.

In the China Inland Mission, when the number of missionaries had gone up to 200, at a conference held in China they felt so deeply the need of more laborers for districts quite unprovided for, that after much prayer they felt at liberty to ask God to give them within a year 100 additional laborers and L10,000 to meet the expenses. They agreed to continue in prayer day by day throughout the year. At the end of the time the 100 suitable men and women had been found, with L11,000.

To meet the need of the world, its open fields, and its waiting souls, the churches all complain of the lack of laborers and of funds. Does not Christ's voice call us to the united and unceasing prayer of the first disciples? God is faithful, by the power of his Spirit, to supply every need. Let the Church take the posture of united prayer and supplication. God hears prayer.

Lord, teach your Church what it means to so much live and labor for you, in the spirit of unceasing prayerfulness, that our faith may rise to the assurance that you will indeed, in a way surpassing all expectation, meet the crying need of a dying world. Amen.

17 Intercession for Individual Souls
You will be gathered one by one, O people of Israel. (Is 27:12)

In our body every member has its appointed place. So, too, in society and in the Church. The work must always aim at the welfare and the highest perfection of the whole, through the cooperation of every individual member.

Too often, in the Church the thought is found that the salvation of men is the work of the minister; yet he generally only deals with the crowd and seldom reaches the individual. This causes a twofold evil. The individual believer does not understand that it is necessary for him to testify to those around him—for the nourishment and the strengthening of his own spiritual life, and for the ingathering of souls. Unconverted souls suffer unspeakable loss because Christ is not personally brought to them by each believer they meet. The thought of intercession for those around us is all too seldom found. Its restoration to its right place in the Christian life—how much that would mean to the Church and its missions!

"What God in heaven desires to do needs prayer on earth as its indispensable condition." As we realize this, we will understand that intercession is the chief element in the conversion of souls. All our efforts are vain without the power of the Holy Spirit given in answer to prayer. It is when ministers and people unite in a covenant of prayer and testimony that the Church will flourish and that every believer will understand the part he has to take.

What can we do to stir up the spirit of intercession? There is a twofold answer. Let every Christian, as he begins to get an insight into the need and the power of intercession, begin to exercise it on behalf of single individuals. Pray for your children, for your relatives and friends, for all with whom God brings you into contact. If you feel that you have not the power to intercede, let the discovery humble you and drive you to the mercyseat. God wants every redeemed child of his to intercede for those who don't know him. It is the vital breath of the normal Christian life—the proof that it is born from above.

Then pray fervently and persistently that God may give the power of his Holy Spirit to you and his children around you so that the power of intercession may have the place that God will honor.

18 Intercession for Ministers
And also for me. (Eph 6:19) *Pray also for us.* (Col 4:3) *Finally, brethren, pray for us.* (2 Thes 3:1)

These expressions of Paul suggest how convinced he was that the Christians had power with God, and that their prayer would indeed bring new strength to him in his work. He had such a sense of the actual unity of the body of Christ, of the interdependence of each member, even the most honorable, on the life that flowed through the whole body, that he sought to rouse Christians, for their own sakes, and for his sake, and for the sake of the kingdom of

God, with his call: "Continue in prayer, and watch in the same with thanksgiving, praying also for us."

The Church depends upon the ministry to an extent that we very little realize. The place of the minister is so high, as the steward of the mysteries of God, as the ambassador for God to beseech men in Christ's name to be reconciled to him, that unfaithfulness or inefficiency brings a terrible blight on the Church that he serves. If Paul, after having preached for twenty years in the power of God, still needed the prayer of the Church, how much more does the ministry in our day need it?

The minister needs the prayer of his people. He has a right to it. He is dependent on it. It is his task to train Christians for their work of intercession on behalf of the Church and the world. He must begin with training them to pray for himself. He may have to begin still farther back and learn to pray more for himself and for them. Let all intercessors who are seeking to enter more deeply into their work give a larger place to the ministry, whether of their own church or of other churches.

Let them plead with God for individual men and for special circles. Let them continue in prayer and watch, that ministers may be men of power, men of prayer, and full of the Holy Spirit. Pray for the ministry!

Father in heaven, arouse believers to a sense of their calling to pray for the ministers of the gospel in the spirit of faith. Amen.

19 Prayer for All Saints
Pray at all times in the Spirit, with all prayer and supplication. To that end keep alert with all perseverance, making supplication for all the saints. (Eph 6:18)

Notice how Paul repeats the words in the intensity of his desire to reach the hearts of his readers. "With *all* prayer and supplication . . . keep alert with *all* perseverance and making supplication for *all* the saints." It is "all prayer, all perseverance, for all the saints. The words need thought, if they are to meet with the needed response.

Paul felt so deeply the unity of the body of Christ and was

so sure that that unity could only be realized in the exercise of love and prayer, that he pleaded with the believers at Ephesus unceasingly and fervently to pray for all saints— not only those in their immediate circle, but in all the Church of Christ of whom they might hear. "Unity is strength." As we exercise this power of intercession with all perseverance, we will be delivered from self with all its feeble prayers and lifted up to that enlargement of heart in which the love of Christ can flow freely and fully through us.

Often, the great lack in true believers is that in prayer they are occupied with themselves and with what God must do for them. Realize that God calls every believer to give himself without ceasing to the exercise of love and prayer. As we forget ourselves, in the faith that God will take care of us, and yield ourselves to the great work of calling down the blessing of God on others, the whole Church will be equipped to do its work of making Christ known to every creature. This alone is the healthy and the blessed life of a child of God who has yielded himself wholly to Christ Jesus.

Pray for God's children and the Church around you. Pray for all the work in which they are engaged, or ought to be. Pray at all seasons in the Spirit for all God's saints. There is nothing greater than abiding communion with God, and nothing that leads to this more surely than the life of intercession for which these words of Paul appeal so pleadingly.

20 Missionary Intercession
Then after fasting and praying they laid their hands on them and sent them off. (Acts 13:3)

"How to multiply the number of Christians, who will individually and collectively wield this force of intercession for the conversion and transformation of men, that is the supreme question of Foreign Missions. Every other consideration and plan is secondary to that of wielding the forces of prayer."

"That those who love this work, and bear it upon their

hearts will follow the scriptural injunction to pray unceasingly for its triumph, we take for granted. To such, not
only the Morning Watch and the hours of stated devotion,
but all times and seasons will witness an attitude of
intercession that refuses to let God go until he crowns his
workers with victory."

Missions are rooted in the love of Christ, as that was
proved on the cross and now lives in our heart. As men
earnestly seek to carry out God's plans for the natural
world, so God's children should be at least as wholehearted
in seeking to bring Christ's love to all mankind. Intercession is the chief means appointed by God to bring the
great redemption within the reach of all.

Pray for missionaries, that the Christ-life may be clear
and strong, that they may be men and women of prayer and
filled with love, in whom the power of the spiritual life is
made manifest.

Pray for native Christians, that they may know the glory
of the mystery in their own countries, Christ in them the
hope of glory.

Pray for all the pupils in missionary schools, that the
teaching of God's Word may be in power. Pray especially
for the native pastors and evangelists, that the Holy Spirit
may fill them to be witnesses for Christ to others.

Pray, above all, for the Church of Christ, that it may be
lifted out of its indifference, and that every believer may
understand that the one object of his life is to help to make
Christ King on the earth.

*Our gracious God, we look to you. In mercy hear our prayer and
by the Holy Spirit reveal the presence and the power of Christ in
the work of your servants. Amen.*

21 The Grace of Intercession
*Continue steadfastly in prayer, being watchful in it
with thanksgiving; and pray for us also.* (Col 4:2, 3)

Nothing can bring us nearer to God and lead us deeper into
his love than the work of intercession.

Nothing can give us a higher experience of the likeness of

God than the power of pouring out our hearts into the bosom of God, in prayer for men around us. Nothing can so closely link us to Jesus Christ, the great Intercessor, and give us the experience of his power and Spirit resting on us, as yielding our lives to the work of bringing the great redemption into the hearts and lives of others. There is nothing in which we can know more of the powerful working of the Holy Spirit than the prayer breathed by him into our hearts, "Abba, Father," in all the fullness of meaning that it had for Christ in Gethsemane. Nothing can so help us to prove the power and the faithfulness of God to his Word, as when we reach out in intercession to the multitudes, either in the Church of Christ or outside it. As we pour out our souls as a living sacrifice before God, with the one persistent plea that he, in answer to our prayer, open the windows of heaven and send down his abundant blessing, God will be glorified, our souls will reach their highest destiny, and God's kingdom will come.

Nothing will so help us to understand and to experience the living unity of the body of Christ and the irresistible power that it can exert, as the daily and continued fellowship with God's children in the persistent plea that God will arise and have mercy upon Zion and make her a light and a life to those who are sitting in darkness. How little we realize what we are losing in not living in fervent intercession! What may we not gain for ourselves and for the world if we allow God's Spirit, as a Spirit of grace and of supplication, to master our whole being!

In heaven Christ lives to pray; his whole communion with his Father is prayer; an asking and receiving of the fullness of the Spirit for his people. God delights in nothing so much as in prayer. Shall we not learn to believe that the highest blessings of heaven will be unfolded to us as we pray more?

Father, pour down the Spirit of supplication and intercession on your people. Amen.

22 United Intercession
There is one body and one Spirit. (Eph 4:4)

Our own bodies teach us how essential for their health and strength it is that every member should take its full share in seeking the welfare of the whole. It is even so in the body of Christ. There are too many who look upon salvation only in terms of their own happiness. There are those, again, who know that they do not live for themselves, and who truly seek in prayer and work to bring others to share in their happiness; but they do not yet understand that in addition to their personal circle or Church, they are called to enlarge their hearts to take the whole body of Christ Jesus into their love and their intercession.

Yet this is what the Spirit and the love of Christ will enable them to do. It is only when intercession for the whole Church, by the whole Church, ascends to God's throne, that the Spirit of unity and of power can have its full sway. The desire that has been awakened for closer union between the different branches of the Church of Christ is cause for thanksgiving. And yet the difficulties are so great and, in the case of different nationalities of the world, so apparently insuperable, that the thought of a united Church on earth appears beyond reach.

Praise God that there is a unity in Christ Jesus, deeper and stronger than any visible manifestation could make it; and that there is a way in which even now, amidst all diversity of administrations, the unity can be exemplified and utilized as the means of an unthought-of accession of divine strength and blessing in the work of the kingdom. It is in the cultivation and increase of the spirit and in the exercise of intercession that the true unity can be realized. As believers are taught the meaning of their calling as a royal priesthood, they see that God is not confined in his love or promises to their limited spheres of labor, but invites them to enlarge their hearts. Like Christ—we may say like Paul too—they may pray for all who believe, or can yet be brought to believe, that this earth and the Church of Christ in it will by intercession be bound to the throne of heaven as it has never yet been.

Let Christians and ministers agree and bind themselves together for this worldwide intercession. It will strengthen the confidence that prayer will be heard, and that their prayers too will become indispensable for the coming of the kingdom.

23 Unceasing Intercession
Pray constantly. (1 Thes 5:17)

How different is the standard of the average Christian, with regard to a life in the service of God, from that which Scripture gives us. In the former, the chief thought is personal safety—grace to pardon our sin and to live such a life as may secure our entrance into heaven. How high above this is the Bible's standard—a Christian surrendering himself with all his powers, with his time and thought and love wholly yielded to the glorious God who has redeemed him, and whom he now delights in serving, in whose fellowship is heaven begun.

To the former the command, "Pray constantly," is simply a needless and impossible life of perfection. Who can do it? We can get to heaven without it. To one who really believes, on the contrary, it promises the highest happiness, a life crowned by all the blessings that can be brought down on souls around through intercession. And as he or she perseveres it becomes increasingly his highest aim upon earth, his highest joy, his highest experience of the wonderful fellowship with the holy God.

"Pray constantly." Let us take that word in a large faith, as a promise of what God's Spirit will work in us, of how close and intimate our union to the Lord Jesus can be, and our likeness to him in his intercession at the right hand of God. Let it become to us one of the chief elements of our heavenly calling, to be consciously the stewards and administrators of God's grace to the world around us. As we think of how Christ said, "I in them, and you in me," let us believe that just as the Father worked in him, so Christ, the interceding High Priest, will work and pray in us. As the faith of our high calling fills our hearts, we shall literally begin to feel that there is nothing on earth to be compared with the privilege of being God's priests, walking without intermission in his holy presence, bringing the burden of the souls around us to the footstool of his throne, and receiving at his hands the power and blessing to dispense to others.

This is indeed the fulfillment of the word of old, "Man created in the likeness and the image of God."

24 Intercession, the Link between Heaven and Earth
Thy will be done, on earth as it is in heaven.
(Mt 6:10)

When God created heaven and earth, he meant heaven to be the divine pattern to which earth was to be conformed; "On earth as it is in heaven" was to be the law of its existence.

The word calls us to think of what constitutes the glory of heaven. God is all in all there. Everything lives in him and to his glory. As we think of what this earth has now become, with all its sin and misery, with the great majority of the race without any knowledge of the true God and the remainder nominally Christians, yet for the greater part utterly indifferent to his claims and estranged from his holiness and love, we feel what a revolution, what a miracle is needed, if the word is to be fulfilled: "On earth as it is in heaven."

And how is this ever to come true? Through the prayers of God's children. The Lord teaches us to pray for it. Intercession is to be the great link between heaven and earth. The intercession of the Son, begun upon earth, continued in heaven, and carried on by his redeemed people upon earth, will bring about the mighty change: "On earth as it is in heaven." As Christ said, "I come to do thy will, O God," until he prayed the great prayer in Gethsemane, "Thy will be done," so his redeemed ones who yield themselves fully to his mind and Spirit make his prayer their own, and unceasingly send up the cry, "Thy will be done, on earth as it is in heaven."

Every prayer of a parent for a child, of a believer for the saving of the lost, or for more grace to those who have been saved, is part of the great unceasing cry going up day and saved, is part of the great unceasing cry going up day and night from this earth, "On earth as it is in heaven."

When God's children learn to pray not only for their immediate circles and interests, but enlarge their hearts to take in the whole Church and the whole world, their united supplication will have power with God and hasten the day when it shall indeed be, "On earth as it is in heaven"—the whole earth filled with the glory of God. Yield yourself, like Christ, to live with this one prayer: "Father, Thy will be done on earth as it is in heaven."

Our Father who art in heaven, hallowed be thy name. Thy kingdom come, thy will be done, on earth as it is in heaven. Amen.

25 The Fulfillment of God's Desires
The Lord ... has desired it [Zion] for his habitation;
"... here I will dwell, for I have desired it." (Ps 132:13, 14)

This is the one great desire of God that moved him in the work of redemption. His heart longed for man, to dwell with him and in him.

To Moses he said, "Let them make me a sanctuary; that I may dwell among them." And just as Israel had to prepare the dwelling for God, even so his children are now called to yield themselves for God to dwell in them, and to win others to become his habitation. As the desire of God towards us fills the heart, it will waken within us the desire to gather others around us to become his dwelling too.

What an honor! What a high calling, to count my worldly business as entirely secondary and to find my life and my delight in winning souls in whom God may find his heart's delight! "Here I will dwell, for I have desired it."

And this is what I can above all do through intercession. I can pray for those around me, asking God to give them his Holy Spirit. It is God's great plan that man himself shall build him a habitation. It is in answer to the unceasing intercession of his children that God will give his power and blessing. As this great desire of God fills us, we will give ourselves wholly to labor for its fulfillment.

Think of David, when he thought of God's desire to

dwell in Israel. He said, "I will not give sleep to my eyes, nor slumber to mine eyelids, until I find out a place for the Lord, an habitation for the mighty God of Jacob." And shall not we, to whom it has been revealed what that indwelling of God may be, give our lives for the fulfillment of his heart's desire?

Let us begin, as never before, to pray for our children, for the souls around us, and for all the world. And that not only because we love them, but especially because God longs for them and gives us the honor of being the channels through whom his blessing is brought down. Realize what it means that God seeks to train us as intercessors, through whom the great desire of his loving heart can be satisfied!

O God, who has said of human hearts, "Here I will dwell, for I have desired it," teach us to pray, day and night, that the desire of your heart may be fulfilled. Amen.

26 The Fulfillment of Man's Desire
Take delight in the Lord, and he will give you the desires of your heart. (Ps 37:4)

God is love, an ever-flowing fountain out of which streams the unceasing desire to make his creatures the partakers of all the holiness and the blessedness there is in himself. This desire for the salvation of souls is indeed God's perfect will, his highest glory.

This loving desire of God, to get his place in the heart of men, he imparts to all his children who are willing to yield themselves wholly to him. It is in this that the likeness and image of God consist—to have a heart in which his love takes complete possession and leads us to spontaneously find our highest joy in loving as he does.

In this way our text is fulfilled: "Take delight in the Lord," and in his life of love, "and he will give you the desires of your heart." The intercession of love, rising up to heaven, will be met with the fulfillment of the desire of our heart. We may be sure that, as we delight in what God delights in, such prayer is inspired by God and will be answered. And our prayer becomes unceasingly, "Your desires, O Father, are mine. Your holy will of love is my will too."

In fellowship with him we get the courage, with our whole will and strength, to bring to him the persons or the circles in which we are interested in an ever-growing confidence that our prayer will be heard. As we reach out in yearning love, we receive the power to take hold of the will of God to bless, and to believe that God will work out his own will in giving us the desire of our hearts, because the fulfillment of his desire has been the delight of our souls.

We then become, in the highest sense of the word, God's fellow-laborers. Our prayer becomes part of God's divine work of reaching and saving the lost, and we learn to find our happiness in losing ourselves in the salvation of those around us.

Father, teach us that nothing less than delighting ourselves in you and in your desires toward men can inspire us to pray and assure us of an answer. Amen.

27 My Great Desire

One thing have I asked of the Lord, that will I seek after; that I may dwell in the house of the Lord all the days of my life, to behold the beauty of the Lord, and to inquire in his temple. (Ps 27:4)

Here we have man's response to God's desire to dwell in us. When the desire of God toward us begins to rule the life and heart, our desire is fixed on one thing, to dwell in the house of the Lord all the days of our life, to behold the beauty of the Lord, to worship him in the beauty of holiness; and then to inquire in his temple and to learn what it means that God has said: "I the Lord have spoken, and I will do it. This also I will let the house of Israel ask me to do for them" (Ez 36:36, 37).

The more we realize the desire of God's love to give his rest in the heart, and the more the desire is awakened in us to dwell every day in his temple and behold his beauty, the more the Spirit of intercession will grow upon us, to claim all that in his New Covenant God has promised. Whether we think of our Church and country, of our home and school, of our nearer or wider circle; whether we think of the saved and all their needs, or the unsaved and their danger, the thought that God is indeed longing to find his home and his rest in the hearts of men, if he be only "inquired of," will rouse our whole being to strive for Zion's sake not to hold our peace. All the thoughts of our feebleness and unworthiness will be swallowed up in the wonderful assurance that he has said of human hearts: "This is my resting place forever; here I will dwell; for I have desired it" (Ps 132:14).

As our faith sees how high our calling is, how indispensable God has made fervent, intense, persistent prayer as the condition of his purpose being fulfilled, we will be drawn to give up our life to a closer walk with God, to an unceasing waiting upon him, and to a testimony to our brothers and sisters of what God will do in them and in us.

Is it not wonderful beyond all thought, this divine partnership, in which God commits the fulfillment of his desires to our keeping? Shame upon us that we have so little realized it!

Father in heaven, give in power the Spirit of grace and supplication to your people. Amen.

28 Intercession Day and Night
And will not God vindicate his elect, who cry to him day and night? Will he delay long over them? (Lk 18:7)

When Nehemiah heard of the destruction of Jerusalem, he cried to God: "Hear the prayer of thy servant which I pray before thy face day and night." Of the watchman set on the walls of Jerusalem, God said, "which shall never hold their peace day nor night." And Paul writes, "Praying earnestly night and day . . . that he may establish your hearts unblamable in holiness before our God and Father" (1 Thes 3:10, 13).

Is such prayer night and day really needed and really possible? Most assuredly, when the heart is so entirely possessed by the desire that it cannot rest until this is fulfilled. The life has so come under the power of the heavenly blessing that nothing can keep it from sacrificing all to obtain it.

When a child of God begins to get a real vision into the need of the Church and of the world, a vision of the divine redemption which God has promised in the outpouring of his love into our hearts, a vision of the power of true intercession to bring down the heavenly blessing, a vision of the honor of being allowed as intercessors to take part in that work, it comes as a matter of course that he regards the work as the most heavenly thing upon earth—as intercessor to cry day and night to God for the revelation of his mighty power.

Let us learn from David, who said, "Zeal for thy house consumes me"; from Christ our Lord, of whom these words were so intensely true, that there is nothing so much worth living for as this one thought—how to satisfy the heart of God in his longing for human fellowship and affection, and how to win hearts to be his dwelling-place. And shall not we too give ourselves no rest until we have found a place for the Mighty One in our hearts and yielded ourselves to the great work of intercession for so many after whom the desires of God are going out.

God grant that our hearts may be so brought under the influence of these divine truths, that we may indeed yield ourselves to make our devotion to Christ and our longing to satisfy the heart of God the chief object of our life.

Lord Jesus, the great Intercessor, who finds in it all your glory, breathe your own Spirit into our hearts. Amen.

29 The High Priest and His Intercession

Consequently he is able for all time to save those who draw near to God through him, since he always lives to make intercession for them. For it was fitting that we should have such a high priest. (Heb 7:25, 26; see also 8:1)

In Israel, what a difference there was between the high priest and the priests and Levites. The high priest alone had access to the Holiest of All. He bore on his forehead the golden crown, "Holiness to the Lord," and by his intercession on the great Day of Atonement he bore the sins of the people. The priests brought the daily sacrifices, stood before the Lord, and came out to bless the people. The difference between high priest and priest was great. But still greater was the unity; they formed one body with the high priest, sharing with him the power to appear before God to receive and dispense his blessing to his people.

The same is true of our great High Priest. He alone has power with God, in a never-ceasing intercession, to obtain from the Father what his people need. And yet, infinite though the distance be between him and the royal priesthood that surrounds him for his service, the unity and the fellowship into which his people have been taken up with him is no less infinite than the apparent diversity. The blessing that he obtains from his Father for us, he holds for his people to receive from him through their fervent supplication, to be dispensed to the souls among whom he has placed them as his witnesses and representatives.

As long as Christians simply think of being saved, and of a life which will make that salvation secure, they never can understand the mystery of the power of intercession to which they are called. But once they realize that salvation means a vital life union with Jesus Christ, an actual sharing of his life dwelling and working in us, and the consecration of our whole being, to live and labor, to think and will, and find our highest joy in living as a royal priesthood, the Church will put on her strength and prove, in fellowship with God and man, how truly the likeness and the power of Christ dwell in her.

May God open our hearts to know and prove what our royal priesthood is—what the real meaning is of our living and praying in the name of Jesus, that what we ask shall indeed be given us! O Lord Jesus, our holy High Priest, breathe the Spirit of your own holy priesthood into our hearts. Amen.

Month Three

1 A Royal Priesthood

Call to me and I will answer you, and will tell you great and hidden things which you have not known. (Jer 33:3)

As you plead for the great mercies of the New Covenant to be bestowed, take with you these thoughts:

1) The infinite willingness of God to bless. His very nature is a pledge of it. He delights in mercy. He waits to be gracious. His promises and the experience of his saints assure us of it.

2) Why then does the blessing so often tarry? In creating man with a free will and making him a partner in the rule of the earth, God limited himself. He made himself dependent on what man would do. Man by his prayer would hold the measure of what God could do in blessing.

3) Think how God is hindered and disappointed when his children do not pray, or pray only little. The low, feeble life of the Church, the lack of the power of the Holy Spirit for conversion and holiness, is all owing to the lack of prayer. How different would be the state of the Church and of the world, if God's people were to take no rest in calling upon him!

4) And yet God has blessed, to the measure of the faith and the zeal of his people. It is not for them to be content with this as a sign of his approval, but rather to say, "If he has thus blessed our feeble efforts and prayers, what will he

not do if we yield ourselves wholly to a life of intercession?"

5) What a call to penitence and confession! Our lack of consecration has kept back God's blessing from the world. He was ready to save men, but we were not willing for the sacrifice of a wholehearted devotion to Christ and his service.

God counts upon you to take your place before his throne as intercessors. Wake up to the consciousness of your holy calling as a royal priesthood. Begin to live a new life in the assurance that intercession, in the likeness and the fellowship with the Lord Jesus in heaven interceding, is the highest privilege a man can desire. In this spirit take up the word with large expectations: "Call to me and I will answer you, and will tell you great and hidden things which you have not known."

Let each of us decide whether we are willing, whether we do not long to give ourselves wholly to this calling, and in the power of Jesus Christ make intercession and supplication for God's Church and people, and for a dying world, the one chief object of our lives. Is this asking too much? Is it too much to yield our lives for this holy service of the royal priesthood, to the One who gave himself for us?

2 Intercession a Divine Reality
And another angel came . . . and he was given much incense to mingle with the prayers of all the saints upon the golden altar before the throne. (Rv 8:3)

Are the thoughts in this book a sufficiently grave indictment of the subordinate place given to intercession in the teaching and practice of the Church, with its ministers and members? Is it not indeed of such supreme importance to make intercession an essential, altogether indispensable element in the true Christian life? To those who take God's Word in its full meaning, there can be no doubt about the answer.

Intercession is, by amazing grace, an essential element in God's redeeming purpose—so much so that without it the failure of its accomplishment may lie at our door. Christ's intercession in heaven is essential to his carrying out of the work he began upon earth, but he calls for the intercession of the saints in the attainment of his object. "All this is of God, who through Christ reconciled us to himself and gave us the ministry of reconciliation." As the reconciliation depended on Christ doing his part, so in the accomplishment of the work he calls on the Church to do her part. Paul regarded intercession day and night as indispensable to the fulfillment of the work that had been entrusted to him. It is only one aspect of that mighty power of God which works in the heart of his believing people.

Intercession is indeed a divine reality. Without it, the Church loses one of its chief beauties, the joy and the power of the Spirit life for achieving great things for God. Without it, the command to preach the gospel to every creature can never be carried out. Without it, there is no power for the Church to recover from her sickly, feeble life and conquer the world. And in the life of the believer, minister, or member, there can be no entrance into the abundant life and joy of daily fellowship with God, except as he takes his place among God's elect—the watchmen and remembrancers of God, who cry to him day and night.

Church of Christ, awake, awake! Listen to the call, "Pray without ceasing": Take no rest, and give God no rest. Let the answer be, even though it be with a sigh from the depths of the heart, "For Zion's sake, will I not hold my peace." God's Spirit will reveal to us the power of a life of intercession as a divine reality, an essential and indispensable element of the great redemption and therefore also of the true Christian life.

May God help us to know and to fulfill our calling!

3 True Worship
Worship God. (Rv 22:9)

Perhaps you have asked, "Why are prayer and intercession not a greater joy and delight? And is there any way in which we may be able to make fellowship with God our chief joy, and as intercessors to bring down his power and blessing on those for whom we pray?"

There may be more than one answer to the question, but

the chief answer is undoubtedly this: We know God too little. In our prayer, his presence is not waited for as the chief thing on which our heart is set. And yet it should be so. We think mostly of ourselves, our need, and weakness, our desire and prayer. But we forget that in every prayer God must be first, must be all. To seek him, to find him, to tarry in his presence, to be assured that his holy presence rests upon us, that he actually listens to what we say, and is working in us—it is this alone that gives the inspiration that makes prayer as natural and easy to us as is the fellowship of a child with his father.

And how is one to attain to this nearness to God and fellowship with him? *We must give God time to make himself known to us.* Believe with all your heart that as you present yourself to God as a supplicant, God presents himself to you as the Hearer of prayer. But you cannot realize this unless you give him time and quiet. It is not the multitude or the earnestness of your words in which prayer has its power, but in the living faith that God himself is taking you and your prayer into his loving heart. He himself will assure you that in his time your prayer will be heard.

The object of this book is to help you to know how to meet God this way in every prayer. Use the texts to help your heart bow before God, waiting on him to make them living and true in your experience.

Begin this day with these words: "To thee, O Lord, do I lift up my soul." Bow before him in stillness, believing that he looks on you and will reveal his presence.

"My soul thirsts for God, for the living God."

4 God Is a Spirit
God is spirit, and those who worship him must worship in spirit and truth. (Jn 4:24)

When God created man, and breathed his own spirit into him, man became a living soul. The soul stood midway between the spirit and the body and had either to yield to the spirit to be lifted up to God, or to the flesh and its lusts. In the Fall, man refused to listen to the spirit and became the slave of the body. The spirit in man became utterly darkened.

In regeneration it is this spirit that is quickened and born again from above. In the regenerate life and in the fellowship with God it is the spirit of man that has ever to yield itself to the Spirit of God. The spirit is the deepest, most inward part of the human being. As we read in Psalm 51:6: "Thou desirest truth in the inward being; therefore teach me wisdom in my secret heart"; or in Jeremiah 31:33: "I will put my law in their inward parts" (KJV). It is of this also that Isaiah says, "My soul yearns for thee in the night, my spirit within me earnestly seeks thee." The soul must sink down into the depths of the hidden spirit, and call upon that to stir itself to seek God.

God is a Spirit, most holy and most glorious. He gave us a spirit with the one object of holding fellowship with himself. Through sin that power has been darkened and nearly quenched. There is no way to restore it but to present the soul in stillness before God for the working of his Holy Spirit in our spirit. Deeper than our thoughts and feelings, God will in our inward part, in our spirits within us, teach us to worship him in spirit and in truth.

"The Father seeketh such to worship him." He himself by the Holy Spirit will teach us this if we wait upon him. In this quiet hour, be still before God, and yield yourself with the whole heart to believe in and to receive the gentle working of his Spirit. And pray such words as these:

"For God alone my soul waits in silence."

"My soul yearns for thee in the night, my spirit within me earnestly seeks thee."

"On Thee, O God, do I wait."

5 Intercession and Adoration
Worship the Lord in holy array. (Ps 96:9)

The better we know God the more wonderful becomes our insight into the power of intercession. We begin to understand that it is the great means by which man can take part in the carrying out of God's purpose. God has entrusted the whole of his redemption in Christ to his people to make known and to communicate to men. In all this, intercession is the chief and essential element, because it is in it that his servants enter into full fellowship with

Christ and receive the power of the Spirit and of heaven as their power for service.

It is easy to see why God has ordered it so. Indeed God desires to renew us after his image and likeness. And there is no other way to do this but by our making his desires our own, so that we breathe his disposition, and in love sacrificing ourselves, so that we may become, in a measure, even like Christ, "ever living to make intercession." Such can be the life of the consecrated believer.

The clearer the insight into this great purpose of God, the more we will desire to enter very truly into God's presence in the spirit of humble worship and holy adoration. The more we thus take time to abide in God's presence, to enter fully into his mind and will, to get our whole soul possessed by the thought of his glorious purpose, the stronger will our faith become that God will himself work out all the good pleasure of his will through our prayers. As the glory of God shines upon us, we will become conscious of the depths of our helplessness, and so rise up into the faith that believes that God will do more than we can ask or think.

Intercession will lead to feeling the need of a deeper adoration. Adoration will give new power for intercession. A true intercession and a deeper adoration will ever be found to be inseparable.

The secret of true adoration can only be known by the soul that waits in God's presence, yielding itself to God for him to reveal himself. Adoration will indeed equip us for the great work of making God's glory known.

"Oh, come let us worship and bow down, let us kneel before the Lord our maker; for he is our God."

"Give to the Lord the glory due his name."

6 The Desire for God
My soul yearns for thee in the night. (Is 26:9)

What is the chief thing, the greatest and most glorious that man can see or find upon earth? Nothing less than God himself.

And what is the chief and the best and the most glorious thing that a man needs every day, and can do every day? Nothing less than to seek and to know, to love and to praise this glorious God. As glorious as God is, so is the glory which begins to work in the heart and life of the man who gives himself to live for God.

What is the first and the greatest thing you have to do every day? Nothing less and nothing greater than to seek this God, to meet him, to worship him, to live for him and for his glory. It is a great step in advance in the life of a Christian when he truly sees this and yields himself to consider fellowship with God every day as the chief end of his life.

The highest wisdom and the one thing for which a Christian is above all to live is to know his God and to love him with his whole heart. Do believe that it is not only indeed true, but that God himself greatly desires that you should live this way with him and will, in answer to prayer, enable you to do so.

Begin today and take a word from God's Book to speak to him in stillness of soul.

"O God, thou art my God, I seek thee, my soul thirsts for thee; my flesh faints for thee" (Ps 63:1).

"With my whole heart I seek thee" (Ps 119:10).

Repeat these words in deep reverence and childlike longing until their spirit and power enter your heart; and wait upon God until you begin to realize the blessedness of thus meeting with him. As you persevere you will learn to expect that the fear and the presence of God can abide with you through all the day.

"I waited patiently for the Lord; he inclined to me and heard my cry" (Ps 40:1).

7 Silent Adoration
For God alone my soul waits in silence. . . . for my hope is from him. (Ps 62:1, 5)

When man in his littleness and God in his glory meet, we all understand that what God says has infinitely more worth than what man says. And yet our prayer so often consists in the utterance of our thoughts of what we need, that we give God no time to speak to us. Our prayers are often indefinite and vague. It is a great lesson to learn—to be silent before God is the secret of true adoration. Let us remember the promise, "In quietness and confidence shall be your strength."

"For God alone my soul waits in silence . . . for my hope is from him" (Ps 62:1).

"I will wait for the Lord; my soul doth wait, and in his word do I hope."

As the soul bows itself before him, remembering his greatness and his holiness, his power and his love, and giving him the honor and the reverence and the worship that are his due, the heart will be opened to receive the divine impression of the nearness of God and of the working of his power.

Such worship of God—in which you bow low and ever lower in your nothingness, and lift up your thoughts to realize God's presence as he gives himself to you in Christ Jesus—is the sure way to give him the glory that is his due, and it will lead to the highest blessedness to be found in prayer.

Do not imagine that it is time lost. Do not turn from it, if at first it appears difficult or fruitless. Be assured that it brings you into the right relationship with God. It opens the way to fellowship with him. It leads to the assurance that he is looking on you in tender love and working in you with a secret but divine power. As at length you become more accustomed to it, it will give you the sense of his presence abiding with you all the day. It will make you strong to testify for God. Someone has said, "No one is able to influence others for goodness and holiness, beyond the amount that there is of God in him." Men will begin to feel that you have been with God.

"The Lord is in his holy temple; let all the earth keep silence before him" (Hab 2:20).

"Be silent, all flesh, before the Lord; for he has roused himself from his holy dwelling" (Zec 2:13).

8 The Light of God's Countenance
God is light. (1 Jn 1:5)
The Lord is my light. (Ps 27:1)

Every morning the sun rises, and we walk in its light and perform our daily duties with gladness. Whether we think of it or not, the light of the sun shines on us all day.

Every morning the light of God shines upon his children. But in order to enjoy the light of God's countenance, the soul must turn to God and trust him to let his light shine upon it.

When there is a shipwreck at midnight, with what longing the mariners look for the morning! How often the sigh goes up, when will the day break? Even so must the Christian wait upon God and rest patiently until his light shines upon him.

"My soul waits for the Lord more than watchmen for the morning" (Ps 130:6).

Begin each day with one of these prayers:

"Let thy face shine on thy servant" (Ps 31:16).

"Lift up the light of thy countenance upon us, O Lord!" (Ps 4:6).

"Let thy face shine, that we may be saved" (Ps 80:3, 7, 19).

Do not rest until you know that the light of his countenance and his blessing is resting on you. Then you will experience the truth of the word: "Blessed are the people . . . who walk, O Lord, in the light of thy countenance, who exult in thy name all the day" (Ps 89:15, 16).

The Father ardently longs for you to dwell in and rejoice in his light all day. Just as you need the light of the sun each hour, so the heavenly light, the light of the countenance of the Father, is indispensable. As surely as we receive and enjoy the light of the sun, so may we confidently count on it that God longs to let his light shine on us.

Even when there are clouds, we still have the sun. So in the midst of difficulties the light of God will rest upon you without ceasing. If you are sure that the sun has risen, you count upon the light all the day. Make sure that the light of God shines upon you in the morning; you can count upon that light being with you all day.

Do not rest until you have said, "There be many that say 'Who will show us any good?' Lord, lift thou up the light of thy countenance upon us." Take time until that light shines in your heart and you can truly say, "The Lord is my light and my salvation" (Ps 27:1).

9 Faith in God
Jesus answered them, "Have faith in God." (Mk 11:22)

As the eye is the organ by which we see the light and rejoice in it, so faith is the power by which we see the light of God and walk in it.

Man was made for God, in his likeness, his whole being formed after the divine pattern. Just think of his wonderful power to think out the thoughts of God hidden in nature. Think of the heart, with its powers of self-sacrifice and love. Man was made for God, to seek him, to find him, to grow up into his likeness and show forth his glory—in the fullest sense to be his dwelling. And faith is the eye which, turning away from the world and self, looks to God and in his light sees light. To faith God reveals himself.

How often we toil and try to waken thoughts and feelings concerning God which are but a faint shadow, forgetting "to gaze on the Incomparable Original." Could we but realize it, in the depth of our soul God reveals himself.

Without faith it is impossible to please God or to know him. In our quiet time we pray to our Father who is in secret. There "he hides us in the secret of his pavilion." And there, as we wait and worship before him, he will indeed let his light shine into our heart, just as light by its very nature reveals itself.

Let our one desire be to take time to be still before God, believing with an unbounded faith in his longing to reveal himself to us. Let us feed on God's Word, which strengthens our faith. And let that faith have large thoughts of what God's glory is, of his power to reveal himself to us, of his longing love to take complete possession of us.

Such faith, exercised and strengthened day by day in secret fellowship with God, will become the habit of our life, keeping us ever in the enjoyment of his presence and the experience of his saving power.

"Abraham grew strong in his faith as he gave glory to God, fully convinced that God was able to do what he had promised" (Rom 4:20, 21).

"I have faith in God that it will be exactly as I have been told" (Acts 27:25).

"Wait for the Lord; be strong, and let your heart take courage; yea, wait for the Lord!" (Ps 27:14).

10 Alone with God
Now it happened that as he was praying alone . . . (Lk 9:18)
Jesus withdrew again to the mountain by himself. (Jn 6:15)

Man needs God. God made him for himself, to find life and happiness in God alone.

Man needs to be alone with God. In his fall he was brought, through the lust of the flesh and the world, under the power of things visible and temporal. His restoration is meant to bring him back to the Father's house, the Father's presence, the Father's love and fellowship. Salvation means being brought to love and to delight in the presence of God.

Man needs to be alone with God. Without this, God has no opportunity to shine into his heart, to transform his nature by his divine working, to take possession and to fill him with the fullness of God.

Man needs to be alone with God, to yield to the presence and the power of his holiness, of his life, and of his love. Christ on earth needed it; he could not live the life of a Son here in the flesh, without at times separating himself entirely from his surroundings and being alone with God. How much more must this be indispensable to us!

When our Lord Jesus commanded us to enter our inner chamber, shut the door, and pray to our Father in secret, he promised that the Father would hear such prayers and answer them in our life before men.

Alone with God—that is the secret of true prayer; of true power in prayer; of real, living, face-to-face fellowship with God; and of power for service. There is no true, deep conversion, no true, deep holiness, no clothing with the Holy Spirit and with power, no abiding peace or joy, *without being daily alone with God.* "There is no path to holiness, but in being much and long alone with God."

What an inestimable privilege is the institution of daily, secret prayer to begin every morning. Let this be the one thing our hearts are set on: seeking, finding, and meeting God.

Take time to be alone with God. You will one day be amazed at the thought that five minutes could be considered enough.

"Hearken to the sound of my cry, my King and my God, for to thee do I pray" (Ps 5:2).

"O Lord, in the morning thou dost hear my voice; in the morning I prepare a sacrifice for thee, and watch" (Ps 5:3).

11 Wholly for God
Whom have I in heaven but thee? And there is nothing upon earth that I desire beside thee. (Ps 73:25)

Alone with God—this is a word of the deepest importance. May we seek grace from God to reach its depths. Then will we learn another word of equally deep significance—wholly for God.

As we find that it is not easy to persevere in being "alone with God," we realize that it is because the other is lacking: we are not "wholly for God." Because he is the only God, God has a right to demand that he should have us wholly for himself. Without this surrender he cannot reveal his power. We read in the Old Testament that his servants Abraham, Moses, Elijah, and David gave themselves wholly and unreservedly to God, so that he could work out his plans through them. It is only the fully surrendered heart that can fully trust God for all he has promised.

Nature teaches us that if anyone desires to do a great work he must give himself wholly to it. This law is especially true of the love of a mother for her child. She gives herself wholly to the little one whom she loves. Is it not reasonable that the great God of love should have us wholly for himself? Should we not take the watchword, "Wholly for God," as the keynote for our devotions every morning as we rise? As wholly as God gives himself to us, so wholly he desires that we give ourselves to him.

Meditate on these things alone with God, and with earnest desire ask him to work in us, by his almighty power, all that is pleasing in his sight.

Wholly for God! What a privilege. What wonderful grace to equip us for it. Wholly for God! What separation from men, and work, and all that might draw us away from him. Wholly for God! What ineffable blessedness as we learn what it means and what God gives with it.

"You shall love the Lord your God with all your heart, and with all your soul, and with all your might" (Dt 6:5; see also Mt 22:37).

"They . . . had sought him with their whole desire, and he was found by them" (2 Chr 15:15).

"With my whole heart I seek thee" (Ps 119:10).

12 The Knowledge of God
This is eternal life, that they know thee. (Jn 17:3)

The knowledge of God is absolutely necessary for the spiritual life. It is life eternal. Not the intellectual knowledge we receive from others or through our own power of thought, but the living, experiential knowledge in which God makes himself known to us. Just as the rays of the sun on a cold winter's day warm the body, imparting its heat to us, so the living God sheds the life-giving rays of his holiness and love upon the heart that waits on him.

Why do we so seldom experience this life-giving power of the true knowledge of God? Because we do not give God time enough to reveal himself to us. When we pray, we think we know well enough how to speak to God. We forget that one of the very first things in prayer is to be silent before God, that he may reveal himself. By his hidden but mighty power, God will manifest his presence, resting on us and working in us. To know God in the personal experience of his presence and love is life indeed.

Perhaps you have heard of Brother Lawrence. He greatly longed to know God, and for this purpose joined a monastery. His spiritual advisers gave him prayer books to use, but he put them aside. It helps little to pray, he said, if I do not know the God to whom I pray. He believed that God would reveal himself. He remained a long time in silent adoration, in order to come under the full impression of the presence of this great and holy Being. He continued in this practice, until later he lived consciously and constantly in God's presence and experienced his nearness and keeping power. As the sun rising each morning is the pledge of light through the day, so the quiet time waiting upon God, yielding ourselves to his light, will be the pledge of his presence and his power resting with us all day. See that you are sure the sun has risen upon your soul. As the sun on a cold day shines on us and imparts its warmth, believe that the living God will work in you with his love and his almighty power. God will reveal himself as life and light and joy and strength to the soul that waits upon him.

"Lift up the light of thy countenance upon us, O Lord" (Ps 4:6).

"Be still, and know that I am God" (Ps 46:10).

13 God the Father
Baptizing them in the name of the Father and of the Son and of the Holy Spirit. (Mt 28:19)

We should remember that the doctrine of the Holy Trinity has a deep devotional aspect. As we think of God we remember the inconceivable distance that separates him in his holiness from sinful men, and we bow in deep contrition and holy fear. As we think of Christ the Son, we remember the inconceivable nearness in which he came to be born of a woman, a daughter of Adam, dying the accursed death, inseparably joined to us to all eternity. And as we think of the Holy Spirit we remember the inconceivable blessedness of God in making us his home and his temple through eternity.

When Christ taught us to say, "Our Father, who art in heaven," he immediately added, "Hallowed be thy name." As God is holy, so we are to be holy. And there is no way of becoming holy but by counting that name most holy and drawing near to him in prayer.

How often we speak that name without any sense of the unspeakable privilege of our relation to God. If we would just take time to come into contact with God and to worship him in his fatherly love, how the inner chamber would become to us the gate of heaven.

When you pray to your Father in secret, bow very low before him and adore his name as most holy. Remember that this is the highest blessedness of prayer.

"Pray to your Father who is in secret; and your Father who sees in secret will reward you" (Mt 6:6).

What an unspeakable privilege, to be alone with God in secret, to say, "My Father"; to know he has seen me in secret and will reward me openly. Take time until you can say, "I have seen God face to face, and yet my life is preserved" (Gn 32:30).

14 God the Son
Grace to you and peace from God our Father and the Lord Jesus Christ. (Rom 1:7)

It is remarkable that the Apostle Paul, in each of his thirteen epistles writes, "Grace to you and peace from God our Father and the Lord Jesus Christ." He had such a deep sense of the inseparable oneness of the Father and the Son in the work of grace, that in each opening benediction he refers to both.

This is a lesson for us of the utmost importance. There may be times in the Christian life when one thinks chiefly of God the Father, and prays to him. But later on we realize that we must grasp the truth that each day and each hour it is only through faith in Christ and in living union with him that we can enjoy a full and abiding fellowship with God.

Remember what we read of the Lamb in the midst of the throne. John had seen One sitting on a throne, "and the four living creatures ... day and night ... never cease to sing,

'Holy, holy, holy, is the Lord God Almighty, who was and is and is to come'" (Rv 4:8).

Later he saw "in the midst of the throne a Lamb as though it had been slain" (Rv 5:6). Of all the worshipping multitude none could see God, but he first saw Christ the Lamb of God. And none could see Christ without seeing the glory of God, the Father and Son inseparably One.

If you would know and worship God, seek him and worship him in Christ. And if you seek Christ, seek him and worship him in God. Then you will understand what it is to have "your life hid with Christ in God," and you will know how indispensable the fellowship and adoration of Christ is to the full knowledge of the love and holiness of God.

Be still and speak these words in deepest reverence: "Grace and peace"—all I could desire—"from God the Father and the Lord Jesus Christ."

Take time to meditate and believe, to expect all from God the Father, who sits upon the throne, and from the Lord Jesus Christ, the Lamb in the midst of the throne. Then you will learn truly to worship God. Return frequently to this sacred scene, to give "to him who sits upon the throne and to the Lamb ... blessing and honor and glory and might for ever and ever!" (Rv 5:13).

15 God the Holy Spirit
Through him we both have access in one Spirit to the Father. (Eph 2:18)

In our communion with God in the inner chamber, we must guard against seeking to know God and Christ in the power of the intellect or the emotions. The Holy Spirit has been given for the express purpose that "we have access in one Spirit ... to the Father." Let us beware lest our labor be in vain, because we do not wait for the teaching of the Spirit.

Christ taught his disciples this truth in the last night. Speaking of the coming of the Comforter, he said, "Ask and you will receive, that your joy may be full." Hold fast the truth that the Holy Spirit was given to teach us to pray. He makes the fellowship with the Father and the Son a reality. Be strong in the faith that he is working secretly in you. As you enter the inner chamber, give yourself wholly to his guidance as your Teacher in all your intercession and adoration.

When Christ said to the disciples on the evening of the resurrection day, "Receive the Holy Spirit," it was, for one thing, to strengthen and equip them for the ten days of prayer and their receiving the fullness of the Spirit. This suggests to us three things we ought to remember when we draw near to God in prayer:

First, we must pray in the confidence that the Holy Spirit dwells in us, and yield ourselves, in stillness of soul, to his leading.

Second, we must believe that the "greater works" of the Spirit for the enlightening and strengthening of the spiritul life—the fullness of the Spirit—will be given in answer to prayer.

Third, we must believe that through the Spirit, in unity with all God's children, we may ask and expect the mighty workings of that Spirit in his Church and people.

"He who believes in me, as the Scripture has said, 'Out of his heart shall flow rivers of living water'" (Jn 7:38).

"Do you believe this?"

16 The Secret of the Lord
But when you pray, go into your room and shut the door and pray to your Father who is in secret; and your Father who sees in secret will reward you. (Mt 6:6)

Christ greatly longed for his disciples to know God as their Father, and for them to have secret fellowship with him. In his own life he found it not only indispensable but the highest happiness to meet the Father in secret. And he would have us realize that it is impossible to be true, wholehearted disciples without daily communion with the Father in heaven, who waits for us in secret.

God is a God who hides himself from the world and all that is of the world. God would draw us away from the world and from ourselves. He offers us instead intimate communion with himself.

Believers in the Old Testament enjoyed this experience:

"Thou art my hiding-place" (Ps 32:7, KJV); "He that dwelleth in the secret place of the Most High shall abide under the shadow of the Almighty" (Ps 91:1, KJV); "The secret of the Lord is with them that fear him" (Ps 25:14, KJV).

How much more should Christians, in the New Covenant, value this secret fellowship with God. We read, "You have died, and your life is hid with Christ in God." If we really believe this, we will have the joyful assurance that our life, hidden with Christ in God, is safely kept and beyond the reach of every foe. Day by day we should confidently seek the renewal of our spiritual life in prayer to our Father, who is in secret.

Because we have died with Christ, one plant with him in the likeness of his death, and also risen with him, we know that, as the roots of a tree are hidden under the earth, so the roots of our daily life are hidden deep in God.

"In the covert of thy presence thou hidest them" (Ps 31:20).

Our first thought in prayer should be this: I must know that I am alone with God and that God is with me.

"He will hide me in his shelter" (Ps 27:5).

17 Half an Hour Silence in Heaven

There was silence in heaven for about half an hour. . . . And another angel came and stood at the altar with a golden censer; and he was given much incense to mingle with the prayers of all the saints upon the golden altar before the throne; and the smoke of the incense rose with the prayers of the saints from the hand of the angel before God.
(Rv 8:1, 3-4)

There was silence in heaven for about half an hour—to bring the prayers of the saints before God, before the first angel sounded his trumpet. And so ten thousands of God's children have felt the absolute need of silence and retirement from the things of earth for half an hour, to present their prayers before God and in fellowship with him to be strengthened for their daily work.

How often the complaint is heard that there is no time for

prayer. And often the confession is made that, even if time could be found, one feels unable to spend the time in real fellowship with God. What hinders growth in the spiritual life? The secret of strength can only be found in living communion with God.

Obey Christ when he says, "When you pray, go into your room and shut the door and pray to your Father who is in secret," and have the courage to be alone with God for half an hour. Do not say, "I will not know how to spend the time." Just believe that if you begin and are faithful, and bow in silence before God, he will reveal himself to you.

If you need help, read some passage of Scripture, and let God's Word speak to you. Then bow in deep humility before God and wait on him. He will work within you. Read Psalms 61, 62, or 63, and speak the words out before God. Then begin to pray. Intercede for your own household and children, for the congregation, for the Church and its leaders, for schools and missions. Keep on, though the time may seem long. God will reward you. But above all, be sure you meet God.

God longs to bless you. Is it not worth the trouble to spend half an hour alone with God? In heaven itself there was need for half an hour's silence to present the prayers of the saints before God. If you persevere, you may find that the half-hour that seems the most difficult in the whole day may at length become the most blessed in your whole life.

"My soul is silent unto God."

"For God alone my soul waits in silence . . . for my hope is from him."

18 God's Greatness
For thou art great and doest wondrous things, thou alone art God. (Ps 86:10)

When anyone commences an important work, he considers the greatness of his undertaking. Scientists, in studying nature, require years of labor to grasp the magnitude of, for instance, the sun and the heavenly bodies.

And is not our glorious God worthy that we should take time to know and adore his greatness.

Yet how superficial is our knowledge of God's greatness. We do not allow ourselves time to bow before him, to come under the deep impression of his incomprehensible majesty and glory.

Meditate on the following texts until you are filled with some sense of what a glorious Being God is.

"Great is the Lord, and greatly to be praised, and his greatness is unsearchable.... I will declare thy greatness.... They shall pour forth the fame of thy abundant goodness" (Ps 145:3, 6-7).

It is not easy to grasp the meaning of these words. Take time for them to master your heart, until you bow, it may be, in speechless adoration before God.

"Ah Lord God! It is thou who hast made the heavens and the earth by thy great power and by thy outstretched arm! Nothing is too hard for thee, ... great in counsel and mighty in deed" (Jer 32:17, 19).

And God answered Jeremiah, "Behold, I am the Lord, the God of all flesh; is anything too hard for me?" (v. 27).

The right comprehension of God's greatness will take time. But if we give God the honor that is his due, and if our faith grows strong in the knowledge of what a great and powerful God we have, we will be drawn to the inner chamber, to bow in humble worship before this great and mighty God. In his abundant mercy he will teach us through the Holy Spirit to say:

"For the Lord is a great God, ... O come, let us worship and bow down, let us kneel before the Lord, our Maker!" (Ps 95:3, 6).

"The Lord is a great God, and a great King above all gods" (Ps 95:3).

19 A Blameless Heart
For the eyes of the Lord run to and fro throughout the whole earth, to show his might in behalf of those whose heart is blameless toward him. (2 Chr 16:9)

We know how important it is in worldly matters to do our work with our whole heart. In the spiritual region this rule still holds good inexorably. God commanded us, "You shall love the Lord your God with all your heart, and with all your soul, and with all your might" (Dt 6:5). And in Jeremiah 29:13, "You will seek me and find me; when you seek me with all your heart."

It is amazing that earnest Christians, who attend to their daily work with all their hearts, are so content to take things easy in the service of God. They do not realize that, if anywhere, they should give themselves to God's service with all the power of their will.

In the words of our text we get an insight into the absolute necessity of seeking God with a blameless and perfect heart. "For the eyes of the Lord run to and fro throughout the whole earth, to show his might in behalf of those whose heart is blameless toward him."

This should encourage us to humbly wait upon God with an upright heart; we may be assured that his eye will be upon us, and he will show forth his mighty power in us and in our work.

Have you learned this lesson in your worship of God—to yield yourself each morning with your whole heart to do God's will? Pray each prayer with a blameless heart, in true, wholehearted devotion to him, and then in faith expect the power of God to work in you and through you.

To come to this, you must begin by being silent before God until you realize that he is indeed working in secret in your heart.

"I wait for my God" (Ps 69:3, KJV).

"He will conceal me under the cover of his tent" (Ps 27:5).

20 The Omnipotence of God
I am God Almighty. (Gn 17:1)

When Abraham heard these words, he prostrated himself. God spoke to him and filled his heart with the faith in what God would do for him. Have you bowed in deep humility before God until you experienced living contact with the Almighty, until your heart has been filled with the faith that he is working in you and will perfect his work in you?

Read in the psalms how the saints of old gloried in God and in his strength.

"I love thee, O Lord, my strength" (Ps 18:1).

"God is the strength of my heart" (Ps 73:26).

"The Lord is the stronghold of my life" (Ps 27:1).

"My strength of soul thou didst increase" (Ps 138:3).

(See also Psalm 18:32; 46:1; 68:28; 118:35; 59:17; 89:17.)

Take time to appropriate these words, and to adore God as the Almighty One, *your* strength.

Christ taught us that salvation is the work of God and quite impossible to man. When the disciples asked, "Who then can be saved?" he answered, "With men this is impossible, but with God all things are possible." If we firmly believe this, we will have the courage to believe that God is working in us all that is pleasing in his sight.

Paul prayed for the Ephesians that through the enlightening of the Spirit they might know "the immeasurable greatness of his power in us who believe, according to the working of his great might." And he prayed that the Colossians would be strengthened with all power, according to his glorious might" (Col 1:11). When we fully believe that the mighty power of God is working without ceasing within us, we can joyfully say, "God is the stronghold of my life."

Do you wonder why many Christians complain of weakness and shortcomings? They do not understand that Almighty God must work in them every hour of the day. That is the secret of the true life of faith.

Do not rest until you can say to God, "I love thee, O Lord, my strength." Let God entirely possess you, and you will be able to say with all God's people, "Thou art the glory of their strength."

21 The Fear of God
Blessed is the man who fears the Lord, who greatly delights in his commandments! (Ps 112:1; see also Ps 128:1, 4)

"The fear of God"—these words characterize the religion of the Old Testament and the foundation which it laid for the more abundant life of the New. "The gift of holy fear" is still the great desire of the child of God and an essential part of a life that is to make a real impression on the world around. It is one of the great promises of the New Covenant in Jeremiah: "I will make an everlasting covenant with them; and I will put the fear of me in their hearts, that they may not turn from me."

We find the perfect combination of the two in Acts 9:31: "The church ... had peace and was built up; and walking in the fear of the Lord and in the comfort of the Holy Spirit it was multiplied." And Paul more than once gives fear a high place in the Christian life. "Work out your own salvation with fear and trembling, for God is at work in you" (Phil 2:12, 13). "Make holiness perfect in the fear of God" (2 Cor 7:1).

The lack of the fear of the Lord is one of the things in which our modern times cannot compare favorably with the times of the Puritans and the Covenanters. No wonder, then, that there is so much cause of complaint in regard to the reading of God's Word, of the worship of his house, and the absence of that spirit of continuous prayer which marked the early Church. We need texts like the one at the head of this reading to be expounded, and for new Christians to be fully instructed in the need and the blessedness of a deep fear of God, leading to an unceasing prayerfulness as one of the essential elements of the life of faith.

Let us earnestly cultivate this grace in the inner chamber. Let us hear the word coming out of the very heavens:

"Who shall not fear and glorify thy name, O Lord? For thou alone art holy."

As we take the word, "Blessed is the man who fears the Lord," into our hearts, we will seek, in every approach to God, to worship him in fear and reverence.

"Serve the Lord with fear, and rejoice with trembling."

22 God Incomprehensible
Behold, God is great, and we know him not. . . . The Almighty—we cannot find him; he is great in power. (Job 36:26; 37:23)

This attribute of God as a Spirit whose being and glory are entirely beyond our power of comprehension is one that we ponder all too little. And yet in the spiritual life it is important to know deeply that, as the heavens are high above the earth, so God's thoughts and ways are infinitely exalted beyond all our thoughts.

With what deep humility and holy reverence we should look up to God and with childlike simplicity yield ourselves to the teaching of his Holy Spirit.

"O the depth of the riches and wisdom and knowledge of God! How unsearchable are his judgments and how inscrutable his ways!" (Rom 11:33).

"O Lord, O God of gods, how wonderful you are in all your thoughts, and how deep your purposes." The study of what God is should fill us with holy awe and with the holy longing to know and honor him rightly.

Consider:

His greatness .... incomprehensible.
His might .... incomprehensible.
His omnipresence .... incomprehensible.
His wisdom .... incomprehensible.
His holiness .... incomprehensible.
His mercy .... incomprehensible.
His love .... incomprehensible.

What an inconceivable glory is in this Great Being who is my God and Father! Confess with shame how little you have sought to know him or to wait upon him to reveal himself. Begin in faith to trust that, in a way passing all understanding, this incomprehensible and all-glorious God will work in your heart and life and give you an ever-growing measure to know him.

"But my eyes are toward thee, O Lord God; in thee I seek refuge" (Ps 141:8).

"Be still, and know that I am God" (Ps 46:10).

23 The Holiness of God in the Old Testament
Be holy, for I am holy.... Be holy; for I the Lord your God am holy. (Lv 11:45; 19:2; see also 20:7, 8; 21:8, 15, 23; 22:9, 16)

Nine times these words are repeated in Leviticus. Israel had to learn that as holiness is the highest and most glorious attribute of God, so it must be the marked characteristic of his people. He who would know God aright, and meet him in secret, must above all desire to be holy as he is holy. The priests who were to have access to God had to be set apart for a life of holiness.

Even so also the prophet who was to speak for him. "I saw the Lord sitting upon a throne, high and lifted up.... The seraphim called to one another: 'Holy, holy, holy is the Lord of hosts'" (Is 6:1-3). The voice of adoration; bow in deep reverence.

"And I said: 'Woe is me! for I am lost; ... for my eyes have seen the King, the Lord of hosts'" (v. 5). The voice of a broken, contrite heart.

Then one of the seraphim touched his mouth with a live coal from off the altar and said: "Your guilt is taken from you, and your sin is forgiven" (v. 7). The voice of grace and full redemption.

Then follows the voice of God: "Whom shall I send?" And the willing answer is, "Here am I, send me." Pause with holy fear, and ask God to reveal himself as the Holy One.

"For thus says the high and lofty One who inhabits eternity, whose name is Holy; 'I dwell in the high and holy place, and also with him who is of a contrite and humble spirit'" (Is 57:15).

Be still and worship God in his great glory and in that deep condescension in which he longs and offers to dwell with us and in us.

If you would meet your Father in secret, bow low and worship him in the glory of his holiness. Give him time to make himself known to you. It is indeed an unspeakable grace to know God as the Holy One.

"Ye shall be holy: for I the Lord your God am holy."

"Holy, holy, holy is the Lord of Hosts."

"Worship the Lord in the beauty of holiness."

"Let the favor of the Lord our God be upon us" (Ps 90:17).

24 The Holiness of God in the New Testament

Keep them in thy name, which thou hast given me.... Sanctify them.... for their sake I consecrate myself, that they also may be consecrated in truth. (Jn 17:11, 17, 19)

Christ ever lives to pray this great prayer. Expect and appropriate God's answer.

Paul says, in 1 Thessalonians, "Praying earnestly night and day that he may establish your hearts unblamable in holiness before our God..." (3:10, 13). "May the God of peace himself sanctify you wholly... He will do it" (5:23, 24).

Ponder these words as you read them, and use them as a prayer: "Lord, establish my heart unblamable in holiness. God himself sanctify me wholly. God is faithful, and he will do it."

What a privilege to commune with God in secret, to speak these words in prayer, and then to wait upon him until through the working of the Spirit they live in our hearts and we begin to know something of the holiness of God.

"To the church of God which is at Corinth, to those sanctified in Christ Jesus, called to be saints..." (1 Cor 1:2).

God's holiness was revealed in the Old Testament. In the New, we find the holiness of God's people in Christ, through the sanctification of the Spirit. He says, "Be holy, for I am holy." For this purpose the Thrice Holy One has revealed himself to us, through the Son and the Holy Spirit. Let us use the word "holy" with great reverence of God, and then with holy desire for ourselves. Worship the God who says, "I am the Lord who sanctify you." Bow before him in holy fear and strong desire, and then, in the fullness of faith, listen to the promise: "God himself sanctify you wholly.... He will do it."

25 Sin
The foremost of sinners. (1 Tm 1:15)
The grace of our Lord overflowed for me with the faith and love that are in Christ Jesus. (1 Tm 1:14)

Never forget for a moment, as you enter the secret chamber, that your whole relation to God depends on what you think of sin, and on what you think of yourself as a redeemed sinner.

It is sin that makes God's holiness so awful. It is sin that makes God's holiness so glorious, because he has said, "Be holy; for I am the Lord your God ... who sanctify you" (Lv 20:7, 8).

It is sin that called forth the wonderful love of God in not sparing his Son. It was sin that nailed Jesus to the cross and revealed the depth and the power of the love with which he loved. Through all eternity in the glory of heaven, it is our being redeemed sinners that will tune our praise.

Never forget for a moment that it is sin that has led to the great transaction between you and Christ Jesus, and that each day in your fellowship with God his one aim is to deliver and keep you fully from its power, and lift you up into his likeness and his infinite love.

It is the thought of sin that will keep you humble at his feet and give the deep undertone to all your adoration. It is the thought of sin, ever surrounding you and seeking to rule you, that will give fervency to your prayer, and urgency to the faith that hides itself in Christ. It is the thought of sin that makes Christ so unspeakably precious, that keeps you every moment dependent on his grace, and gives you the claim to be more than conqueror through him that loved us. It is the thought of sin that calls to us to thank God with the broken and contrite heart which God will not despise, that works in us that contrite and humble spirit in which he delights to dwell.

And it is in the inner chamber, in secret with the Father, that sin can be conquered, the holiness of Christ can be imparted, and the Spirit of holiness take possession of our lives. It is the inner chamber that we will learn to know and experience fully the divine power of the words of promise: "The blood of Jesus his Son cleanses us from all sin. . . . No one who abides in him sins" (1 Jn 1:7; 3:6).

26 The Mercy of God
Oh, give thanks unto the Lord; for he is good: for his mercy endureth for ever." (Ps 136:1, KJV)

This psalm is wholly devoted to the praise of God's mercy. In each of the twenty-six verses we have the expression: "His mercy endureth for ever." The psalmist was full of this glad thought. Our hearts, too, should be filled with the blessed assurance. The everlasting, unchangeable mercy of God is cause for unceasing praise and thanksgiving.

Let us read what is said about God's mercy in the well-known Psalm 103.

"Bless the Lord, O my soul . . . who crowneth thee with lovingkindness and tender mercies" (vv. 1, 4, KJV). Of all God's other attributes, mercy is the crown. May it be a crown upon my head and in my life!

"The Lord is merciful and gracious" (v. 8). As wonderful as God's greatness is, so infinite is his mercy.

"As the heaven is high above the earth, so great is his mercy toward them that fear him" (v. 11, KJV). What a thought! "As the heaven is high above the earth," so immeasurably and inconceivably great is the mercy of God waiting to bestow his richest blessing.

"The mercy of the Lord is from everlasting to everlasting upon them that fear Him" (v. 17). Here again the psalmist speaks of God's boundless lovingkindness and mercy.

How frequently we have read these familiar words without the least thought of their immeasurable greatness! Be still and meditate until the heart responds in the words of Psalm 36:

"Thy mercy, O Lord, is in the heavens" (v. 5).

"How excellent is thy lovingkindness, O God! therefore the children of men put their trust under the shadow of thy wings" (v. 7).

"Oh, continue thy lovingkindness unto them that know thee" (v. 10).

Thank God with great joy for the wonderful mercy with which he crowns your life, saying, "Thy lovingkindness is better than life."

27 The Word of God
The word of God is living and active. (Heb 4:12)

For fellowship with God, his Word and prayer are both indispensable, and in the inner chamber they should not be separated. In his Word, God speaks to me: in prayer, I speak to God.

The Word teaches me to know the God to whom I pray; it teaches me how he would have me pray. It gives me promises to encourage me in prayer, and it often gives me wonderful answers to prayer.

The Word comes from God's heart and brings his thoughts and his love into my heart. And then the Word goes back from my heart into his great heart of love through prayer, the means of fellowship between God's heart and mine.

The Word teaches me God's will—the will of his promises as to what he will do for me, as food for my faith, and also the will of his commands, to which I surrender myself in loving obedience.

The more I pray, the more aware I am of my need of the Word and rejoice in it. The more I read God's Word, the more I have to pray about and the more power I have in prayer. One great cause of prayerlessness is that we read God's Word too little, or only superficially, or in the light of human wisdom.

The Holy Spirit, through whom the Word has been spoken, is also the Spirit of prayer. He will teach me how to receive the Word and how to approach God.

How blessed would the inner chamber be, what a power and an inspiration in our worship, if we only took God's Word as from himself, turning it into prayer, and expecting an answer. The inner chamber, in the secret of God's presence and by the Holy Spirit is where God's Word would become our delight and our strength.

God's Word in deepest reverence in our hearts, and on

our lips, and in our lives, will be a never-failing fountain of strength and blessing.

God's Word is indeed full of a quickening power that will make us strong, joyfully expecting and receiving great things from God. Above all, it will give us the daily fellowship with him as the living God.

"Blessed is the man . . . [whose] delight is in the law of the Lord, and on his law he meditates day and night" (Ps 1:1, 2).

28 The Psalms
How sweet are thy words to my taste, sweeter than honey to my mouth! (Ps 119:103)

Of all the books in the Bible, the book of Psalms is given us especially to help us worship God. The other books are historical, or doctrinal, or practical. But the psalms take us into the inner sanctuary of God's holy presence, to enjoy the blessedness of fellowship with him. It is a book of devotions inspired by the Holy Spirit.

If you would each morning truly meet God and worship him in spirit and in truth, then let your heart be filled with the Word of God in the psalms.

As you read the psalms, underline the word "Lord" or "God," wherever it occurs, and also the pronouns referring to God, "I," "Thou," "He." This will help to connect the contents of each psalm with God, who is the object of all prayer. When you have taken the trouble to mark the different names of God, you will find that more than one difficult psalm will have light shed upon it. These underlined words will make God the central thought and lead you to a new worship of him. Take them upon your lips and speak them out before him. Your faith will be renewed to realize how God is your strength and help in all circumstances of life.

The psalms, as the Holy Spirit taught God's people to pray, will, by the power of that Spirit, teach us, too, ever to abide in God's presence.

Take Psalm 119. Every time that the word "Lord," or "Thou," or "Thy" occurs, underline it. You will be surprised to find that each verse contains these words once, or more than once. Meditate on the thought that the God who is found throughout the whole psalm is the same God who gives us his law and will enable us to keep it.

This psalm will soon become one of the most beloved; you will find its prayers and its teaching concerning God's Word drawing you continually up to God in the consciousness of his power and love.

"Oh, how I love thy law! It is my meditation all the day" (Ps 119:97).

29 The Glory of God
To him be glory. . . to all generations. (Eph 3:21)

God himself must reveal his glory to us; then alone are we able to know and glorify him aright.

There is no more wonderful image in nature of the glory of God than we find in the starry heavens. Telescopes, which are continually made more powerful, have long proclaimed the wonders of God's universe. New wonders of that glory have been revealed by means of photography. A photographic plate fixed below the telescope will reveal millions of stars that could never have been seen by the eye through the best telescope. Man must step to one side and allow the glory of the heavens to reveal itself; then the stars, at first wholly invisible and at immense distances, will leave their image upon the plate.

What a lesson for the soul that longs to see the glory of God in his Word. Put aside your own efforts and thoughts. Let your heart be as a photographic plate that waits for God's glory to be revealed. The plate must be rightly prepared and clean; let your heart be prepared and purified by God's Spirit. "Blessed are the pure in heart, for they shall see God." The plate must be immovable; let your heart be still before God. The plate must be exposed sometimes for seven or eight hours to receive the full impression of the furthest stars; let your heart take time in silent waiting upon God, and he will reveal his glory.

If you keep silence before God and give him time, he will put thoughts into your heart that may be of unspeakable blessing to yourself and others. He will create within you desires and dispositions that will indeed be as the rays of his glory shining in you.

Put this to the proof this morning. Offer your spirit to him in deep humility, and have faith that God will reveal himself in his holy love. His glory will descend upon you. You will yourself feel the need of giving him full time to do his work.

"The Lord is in his holy temple; let all the earth keep silence before him."

"My soul, wait thou only upon God; for my expectation is from him."

"God . . . has shone in our hearts to give the light of the knowledge of the glory of God in the face of Christ" (2 Cor 4:6).

"Be still, and know that I am God."

30 The Holy Trinity
Chosen and destined by God the Father and sanctified by the Spirit for obedience to Jesus Christ and for sprinkling with his blood. (1 Pt 1:2)

The great truth of the Holy Trinity lies at the very root of our spiritual life. In this book we have spoken especially of the adoration of God the Father, and the need of time, sufficient time each day, to worship him. But we must remind ourselves that, for all our communion with God, the presence and the power of the Son and the Spirit are absolutely necessary.

What a field this opens for us in the inner chamber. We need time to realize how all our fellowship with the Father is conditioned by the active and personal presence and working of the Lord Jesus. It takes time to become fully conscious of what need I have of him in every approach to God, what confidence I may have in the work that he is doing for me and in me, and how much I may count upon his presence and all-prevailing intercession. But *it takes time,* and that time will be most greatly rewarded!

Even so with the divine and almighty power of the Holy Spirit working in the depth of my heart, as the One who alone is able to reveal the Son within me. Through him alone I have the power to know what and how to pray; above all, how to plead the name of Jesus and to receive the assurance that my prayer has been accepted.

Does it not now seem almost a mockery to speak of five minutes to be alone with God, to come under the impression of his glory? Does not the thought of the true worship of God in Christ through the Holy Spirit convince you more than ever that it takes time to enter into a holy alliance with God that will keep the heart and mind all the day in his peace and presence? It is in waiting in the secret of God's presence that you receive grace to abide in Christ and all the day to be led by his Spirit.

"Chosen and destined by God the Father and sanctified by the Spirit for obedience to Jesus Christ and for sprinkling with his blood." What food for thought—and worship!

"Thou has said, 'Seek ye my face.' My heart said to thee, 'Thy face, Lord, do I seek.'"

31 The Love of God
God is love, and he who abides in love abides in God, and God abides in him. (1 Jn 4:16)

The best and most wonderful word in heaven is love, for God is love. And the best and most wonderful word in the inner chamber must also be love, for the God who meets us there is love.

What is love? The deep desire to give itself for the beloved. Love finds its joy in imparting all that it has to make the loved one happy. And the heavenly Father, who offers to meet us in the inner chamber, has no other object than to fill our hearts with his love.

All the other attributes of God which have been mentioned find in this their highest glory. The true and full blessing of the inner chamber is nothing less than a life in the abundant love of God.

Take time to meditate in silence on the wonderful revelation of God's love in Christ, until you are filled with the spirit of worship and wonder and longing desire.

Believe that "the love of God has been poured into our hearts by the Holy Spirit which has been given to us."

How little we have believed in, and sought after, this love. And as we pray, let us hold fast this assurance: I am confident that my heavenly Father longs to manifest his love to me. I am deeply convinced of the truth: He will and can do it.

"I have loved you with an everlasting love" (Jer 31:3).

". . . that you, being rooted and grounded in love, may have power to comprehend with all the saints what is the breadth and length and height and depth, and to know the love of Christ which surpasses knowledge" (Eph 3:17, 18, 19).

"See what love the Father has given us" (1 Jn 3:1).

Month Four

1 Waiting upon God
For thee I wait all the day long. (Ps 25:5)

"Waiting upon God." In this expression we find one of the deepest truths of God's Word in regard to the attitude of the soul in its communion with God.

Waiting upon God, that he may reveal himself in us; that he may teach us all his will; that he may do to us what he has promised; that in all things he may be the infinite God.

It is the attitude of soul with which each day should begin. On awaking in the morning, in the inner chamber, in quiet meditation, in the expression in prayer of our ardent longings and desires, in the course of our daily work, in all our striving after obedience and holiness, in all our struggles against sin and self-will—in everything there should be a waiting upon God to receive what he will bestow, to see what he will do, to allow him to be the Almighty God.

Meditate on these things, and they will help you truly to value the precious promises of God's Word.

"They that wait upon the Lord shall renew their strength; they shall mount up with wings as eagles." Here we have the secret of heavenly power and joy.

"Wait on the Lord, be of good courage, and he shall strengthen thine heart; wait, I say, on the Lord."

"Rest in the Lord, and wait patiently for him."

The deep root of all scriptural theology is absolute dependence on God. As we exercise this spirit, it will become more natural and possible to say, "For thee I wait all the day long." And there we have the secret of true, uninterrupted, silent adoration and worship.

"I wait for the Lord, my soul waits, and in his word I hope" (Ps 130:5).

"Be still before the Lord, and wait patiently for him" (Ps 37:7). "And he will give you the desires of your heart" (Ps 37:4).

2 The Praise of God
Praise befits the upright. (Ps 33:1)

Praise will ever be a part of adoration. Adoration, when it has entered God's presence and had fellowship with him, will ever lead to the praise of his name. Let praise be a part of the incense we bring before God in our quiet time.

When the children of Israel, at their birth as the people of God at the Red Sea, had been delivered from the power of Egypt, the joy of redemption in the song of Moses burst forth in this song of praise:

"Who is like unto Thee, O Lord, among the gods? Who is like Thee, glorious in holiness, fearful in praises, doing wonders?"

In the psalms we see what a large place praise ought to have in the spiritual life. There are more than sixty psalms of praise, becoming more frequent as the book draws to its close. See Psalms 95-101, 103-108, 111-118, 134-138, 144-150. The last five are Hallelujah psalms, beginning and ending with "Praise the Lord." And the very last repeats, "Praise him," twice in every verse and ends, "Let everything that breathes praise the Lord."

Let us study this until our whole heart and life be one continual song of praise.

"I will bless the Lord at all times; his praise shall continually be in my mouth." "Every day I will bless thee." "I will sing praises to my God while I have my being."

With the coming of Christ into the world, there was a

new outburst of praise in the song of the angels, the song of Mary, the song of Zechariah, and the song of Simeon.

And then we find in the song of Moses and the Lamb (Rv 15:3, 4) the praise of God filling creation: "Great and wonderful are thy deeds, O Lord God the Almighty! . . . Who shall not fear and glorify thy name . . . For thou alone art holy"; ending (Rv 19:1-6) with the fourfold "Hallelujah! For the Lord our God the Almighty reigns."

Let the inner chamber and the quiet time with God ever lead your heart to unceasing praise.

3 The Image of God
Then God said, "Let us make man in our image, after our likeness." (Gn 1:26)

Here we have the first thought of man—his origin and his destiny entirely divine. God undertook the stupendous work of making a creature, who is not God, to be a perfect likeness of him in his divine glory. Man was to live in entire dependence on God and to receive directly and unceasingly from God himself the inflow of all that was holy and blessed in the Divine Being. God's glory, his holiness, and his love were to dwell in him and shine out through him.

When sin had done its terrible work and spoiled the image of God, the promise was given in Paradise of the seed of the woman, in whom the divine purpose would be fulfilled. "God's Son, who reflects the glory of God and bears the very stamp of his nature" (Heb 1:3), was to become a Son of man, in whom God's plan would be carried out, his image revealed in human form. The New Testament takes up the thought of creation and speaks of those who are "fore-ordained to be conformed to the image of his Son"; of "the new man renewed after the image of his creator"; and promises, "We know that when he shall be manifested, we shall be like him; for we shall see him as he is."

And between the eternal purpose and its eternal realization, we have a wonderful promise regarding life here upon earth. "We all, with unveiled face, beholding the glory of the Lord, are being changed into his likeness from one degree of glory to another; for this comes from the Lord who is the Spirit" (2 Cor 3:18).

It was of this that Paul had said just before: "Shall not the ministration of the Spirit be glorious by reason of the glory that excelleth?" Let us take home the promise of the text as the possible and assured experience for daily life to everyone who gives Christ his place as the Glorified One. Let us set our heart upon the glory of that image of God in Christ, assured that the Spirit will change us into the same image day by day, from glory to glory. Believe firmly and confidently that this promise will be made true in your Christian life. God Almighty, who created man in his image, seeks now to work out his purpose in changing us all into the image of Christ Jesus by the power of the Holy Spirit.

"Let that mind be in you, which was also in Christ Jesus." "I have given you an example, that you also should do as I have done to you."

"Lord, increase our faith."

4 The Obedience of Faith
The Lord appeared to Abram, and said to him, "I am God Almighty; walk before me, and be blameless. And I . . . will multiply you exceedingly." (Gn 17:1, 2)

In Abraham we see how God not only asks for faith and rewards faith, but also how he works faith by the gracious training that he gives. When God first called Abraham, he at once promised him, "By you all the families of the earth shall bless themselves" (Gn 12:3). When he reached the land, God promised that the land should be his (Gn 12:7). And when Abraham returned from the battle against the kings, God again renewed his promise (15:5). Before the birth of Isaac, he sought to strengthen his faith (Gn 17). And once more in the plains of Mamre, he spoke, "Is anything too hard for the Lord?" God led him step by step until his faith was perfected for full obedience in the sacrifice of Isaac. As "by faith Abraham obeyed to go out," so by faith, at the close of forty years, he was able, without any promise, in fact in apparent conflict with all the promises, to obey God's will to the very uttermost.

The Father makes great demands on your faith too. If you are to follow in Abraham's footsteps, you too are to forsake everything and live in the land of spiritual promise, with nothing but his word to depend upon, set apart for God. For this you will need a deep and clear insight that the God who is working in you is the Almighty who will work all his good pleasure. It is not a little thing and easy, to live the life of faith. It requires a life that seeks to abide in his presence all the day. Bow before God in humble worship until he speaks to you too: "I am God Almighty; walk before me, and be blameless. And I will . . . multiply you exceedingly." When Abraham heard this, he "fell on his face: and God talked with him." There you have the secret birthplace of the power to trust God for everything that he promises.

In this book we desire to find out what the power of faith is, and what God is willing to work, "according to the exceeding greatness of his power in us who believe." Only when we are called to a life of true consecration to God and to the complete obedience of faith can we go out like Abraham. Walk in his footsteps. Hide deep in your heart the testimony of God's Word: "He was strong in faith, giving glory to God; being fully persuaded, that what he had promised, he was able to perform."

5 The Love of God
You shall love the Lord your God with all your heart, and with all your soul, and with all your might. (Dt 6:5)

God taught Abraham what it meant to believe in God with all his heart; he was strong in faith, giving glory to God. Moses taught Israel what the first and great commandment was: to love God with all their heart. This first commandment was the origin and fountain out of which the others naturally proceed. It is grounded in the relationship between God, as the loving Creator, and man, made in his image as the object of that love. In the very nature of things it could never be otherwise; man finds his life, his destiny, and his happiness in nothing but just this one thing, loving

God with all his heart, soul, and strength. Moses said, "The Lord set his heart in love upon your fathers" (Dt 10:15); such a God was infinitely worthy of being loved. All our faith in God and obedience to him—our whole life—is to be inspired by this one thought: We are to love God with all our heart, soul, and strength. As children of God, it is our first duty to daily live out this command.

How little Israel was able to obey the command we all know well. But before Moses died, after speaking of the judgments God would bring upon his people for their sins, he made known the promise found in Colossians: "You were circumcised—with a circumcision made without hands, by putting off the body of flesh in the circumcision of Christ" (2:11). He told them, "You will love the Lord your God with all your heart and with all your soul" (Dt 30:6).

This promise was the first indication of the New Covenant, in which, as Jeremiah foretold, the law would be so written in the heart by the Holy Spirit that they would no more depart from God but walk in his ways. But how little have Christians understood this; how easily they rest content with the thought that it is impossible.

Let us learn the double lesson. This blameless heart, loving God with all our might, is what God claims, is what God is infinitely worthy of, is what God—blessed be his name!—will *himself* give and work in us. Let our whole soul go out in faith to meet, to wait for, and to expect the fulfillment of the promise.

"God's love has been poured into our hearts through the Holy Spirit which has been given to us." This assures us of the grace of loving God with all our hearts.

6 The Joyful Sound

Blessed are the people who know the festal shout, who walk, O Lord, in the light of thy countenance, who exult in thy name all the day. (Ps 89:15, 16)

The angel calls the gospel message "glad tidings of great joy." In Psalm 89 it is spoken of as "the joyful sound." That blessedness consists in God's people walking in the light of God and rejoicing in his name all the day. Undisturbed fellowship, never-ending joy, is their portion. Even in the Old Testament the saints at times experienced this. But there was no continuance; the Old Testament could not secure that. Only the New Testament can and does give it.

In every well-ordered family one finds the father delighting in his children and the children rejoicing in their father's presence. And this mark of a happy home on earth is what the Heavenly Father has promised and delights to work in his people; they will walk in the light of his countenance and exult in his name all the day. It has been promised and made possible in Christ through the Holy Spirit filling the heart with the love of God. It is the heritage of all who seek to love God with all their heart and with all their strength.

How many of God's people think it simply impossible and have even given up the hope and the desire for a life of rejoicing in God's presence all the day. And yet Christ clearly promised it: "These things I have spoken to you, that my joy may be in you, and that your joy may be full." "I will see you again and your hearts will rejoice, and no one will take your joy from you."

Consider the Father's longing to have the perfect confidence and love of his children and the children's need of the Father's presence every moment of the day for their happiness and strength. Consider the power of Christ by the Holy Spirit to maintain this life in us. Let us be content with nothing less than knowing the joyful sound, being among those "who walk, O Lord, in the light of thy countenance, who exult in thy name all the day . . . for thou art the glory of their strength."

The more we enter into God's will for us, the stronger our faith will be that the Father can be content with nothing less than his child walking in the light of his countenance and rejoicing in his name all the day; we can be assured that what the Father has meant for us will be wrought in us through Christ and the Holy Spirit.

7 The Thoughts of God
For as the heavens are higher than the earth, so are . . . my thoughts than your thoughts. (Is 55:9)

In his promises of what he will work in us, God reminds us that as high as the heavens are above the earth, so high his thoughts are above ours—altogether beyond our power of spiritual living apprehension.

When he tells us that we are made in the image of God, that by grace we are actually renewed again into that image, and that as we gaze upon God's glory in Christ we are changed into the same image as by the Spirit of the Lord—these are indeed thoughts higher than the heavens. When he told Abraham of all the mighty work he was to do in him, in his seed, and through him in all the nations of the earth, that again was a thought higher than the heavens. Man's mind could not take it in. When God calls us to love him with all our heart, and promises to renew our hearts so we *can* love him with all our strength, this again is a thought out of the very heights of heaven. And when the Father calls us to live in the light of his face and rejoice in his name all the day, we have a gift out of the very depths of his heart of love.

With what deep reverence, humility, and patience should we wait upon God to impart to our hearts through the Holy Spirit the life and the light that makes us feel at home with these thoughts dwelling in us. How necessary is daily, tender, abiding fellowship with God, if we are indeed to enter into his mind, and have his thoughts make their home in us. And what a faith is required to believe that God will not only reveal the beauty and the glory of these thoughts, but will actually so mightily work in us that their divine reality and blessing will fill our inmost being.

Paul quotes Isaiah: "What no eye has seen, nor ear heard, nor the heart of man conceived, what God has prepared for those who love him" (1 Cor 2:9). But God has revealed them to us through the Spirit. When Christ promised his disciples that the Holy Spirit from the throne in heaven should dwell with them, he said that the Spirit would glorify him, and fill us with the light and life of the heavenly world. The Spirit would make him and the purposes of

God, higher than the heavens above the earth, our abiding experience. Realize that every day the Holy Spirit will fill our hearts with the thoughts of God in all their heavenly power and glory.

8 The New Covenant in Jeremiah 31
I will make a new covenant with the house of Israel ... I will put my law within them, and I will write it upon their hearts. (Jer 31:31, 33)

When God made the first covenant with Israel at Sinai, he said, "If you will obey my voice and keep my covenant, you shall be my own possession among all peoples" (Ex 19:5). But Israel had not the power to obey. Their whole nature was carnal and sinful, and there was no provision in the covenant for the grace that should make them obedient. The law only served to reveal their sin.

In our text God promises to make a New Covenant in which men would be able to live a life of obedience. In this New Covenant, the law was to be put in their inward parts and written in their heart, "not with ink, but with the Spirit of the living God," so that they could say with David: "I delight to do thy will, O my God; yea, thy law is within my heart." The law, and delight in it, would, through the Holy Spirit, possess the inner life with all its powers. Or, as we have it in Jeremiah 32:40, after God had said: "Is there anything too hard for me?": "I will make with them an everlasting covenant, ... and I will put the fear of me in their hearts, that they may not turn from me."

In contrast with the Old Testament and its weakness, which made it impossible to be faithful, this promise ensures a continual, wholehearted obedience as the mark of the believer who takes God at his Word and fully claims what the promise secures.

Learn the lesson that in the New Covenant God's mighty power will be shown in the heart of everyone who believes the promise: "They shall not turn from me"; "It shall be even so as it has been spoken unto me." Bow in deep stillness before God and believe what he says. The measure of our experience of this power of God keeping us from departing from him will be in harmony with the law: "According to your faith be it unto you."

We need to be at great pains to keep the contrast between the Old and the New Testament very clear. The Old had a wonderful measure of grace, but not enough for the continual abiding in the faith of obedience. That is the definite promise of the New Testament, the fruit of heart renewal and the power of the Holy Spirit leading the soul and revealing the fullness of grace to keep us "unblamable in holiness."

9 The New Covenant in Ezekiel

I will sprinkle clean water upon you, and you shall be clean from all your uncleannesses, and from all your idols I will cleanse you. A new heart I will give you, and a new spirit I will put within you . . . and cause you to walk in my statutes and be careful to observe my ordinances. (Ez 36:25-27)

Here we have the same promise as in Jeremiah, the promise of such cleansing from sin and such a gift of the Spirit in the new heart, that would secure our walking in God's statutes and keeping his judgments. Just as in Jeremiah God had said: "I will put the fear of me in their hearts, that they may not turn from me," so here: "I will cause you to walk in my statutes and be careful to observe my ordinances." In contrast with the Old Covenant, in which there was no power to enable them to continue in God's law, the great mark of the New Covenant would be a divine power enabling them to walk in his statutes and keep his judgments.

"Where sin abounded, grace did much more abound," working wholehearted allegiance and obedience. Why is this so little experienced? The answer is very simple: The promise is not believed and is not preached; its fulfillment is not expected. Yet how clearly we have it in a passage like Romans 8:1-4. There the man who had complained of the power "bringing him into captivity under the law of sin," thanks God that he is "now in Christ Jesus" and that "the law of the Spirit of life in Christ Jesus has made him free from the law of sin and death," so that the requirement of the law is fulfilled in all who walk in the Spirit.

Once again, why are there so few who can give such testimony, and how can we attain this? Just one thing is needed: faith in an omnipotent God who will by his wonderful power do what he has promised. "I the Lord have spoken it, and will do it." Believe that the promise is true: "You shall be clean from all your uncleannesses ... and I will ... cause you to walk in my statutes." Believe *all* that God here promises, and God will do it. To an extent beyond all power of thought, God has made his great and glorious promises dependent on our faith! The promises will work that faith as we believe them. "According to your faith, be it unto you." This very day, put it to the proof.

10 The New Covenant and Prayer
Call to me and I will answer you, and will tell you great and hidden things which you have not known. (Jer 33:3)
I, the Lord, have spoken, and I will do it.... This also I will let the house of Israel ask me to do for them. (Ez 36:36, 37)

The fulfillment of the great promises of the New Covenant is dependent on prayer. God answered Jeremiah's prayer by saying, "I will put the fear of me in their hearts, that they may not turn from me." And to Ezekiel he had said, "I will cause you to walk in my statues." We do not expect these promises to be truly fulfilled, because of our unbelief and because we judge the meaning of God's Word according to human thought and experience. We do not believe that God means them to be literally true. We do not have the faith that God is waiting to make his promise true in our experience.

God has said that without such faith our experience will be very partial and limited. He has graciously pointed out the way in which such faith can be found, the path of much prayer. "Call to me and I will answer you, and tell you great and hidden things which you have not known." "This also I will let the house of Israel ask me to do for them." When individual men and women turn to God with their whole heart to plead these promises, he will fulfill them. In the exercise of intense persevering prayer, faith will take hold of God and surrender itself to his omnipotent working. And then, as we testify to each other what God has done and will do, we will help each other and take their place as the Church of the living God; we will plead for and firmly expect his promises to be fulfilled in larger measure, as a new enduement for the great work of preaching Christ in the fullness of his redemption to perishing men.

The state of the Church, the state of our ministers and members, and our own state call for unceasing prayer. We need to pray fervently and persistently that the need of the power of the Holy Spirit may be deeply felt, and that a strong faith may be roused in the hearts of many to claim and to expect his mighty working. "I, the Lord, have spoken, and I will do it." "I believe; Lord, help my unbelief."

11 The New Covenant in Hebrews
For I will be merciful toward their iniquities, and I will remember their sins no more. (Heb 8:12)

Christ is called in this epistle the mediator of a better covenant, enacted upon better promises (8:6). In him the two parts of the covenant find their complete fulfillment. First, he came to atone for sin and to destroy its power over man and secure free access to God's presence and favor. And with that came the fuller blessing, the new heart, freed from the power of sin, with God's Holy Spirit breathing into it the delight in God's law and the power to obey it.

These two parts of the covenant may never be separated. And yet how many who put their trust in Christ for the forgiveness of sin, never think of claiming the fullness of the promise, being God's people and knowing him as their God.

Jesus Christ is "the mediator of the New Covenant." The forgiveness of sin is in the power of his blood, and the law is written in the heart through the power of his Spirit. Just as surely as the complete pardon of sin is assured, we may expect the complete fulfillment of the promises, "I will put the fear of me in their hearts, that they may not turn from me"; "I will cause you to walk in my statutes."

God asked Abraham: "I am God Almighty...is anything too hard for me?" He spoke that word to Jeremiah too in regard to the New Covenant. He asks for a strong, wholehearted desire for a life wholly given up to him. We must set aside all our preconceived opinions and in faith believe in the mighty power of God. We must surrender to Jesus Christ as the mediator of the New Covenant, be willing to accept our place with him, crucified to the world and to sin and to self; we must be ready to follow him at any cost. In a word, it means a simple, wholehearted acceptance of Christ as Lord and Master, our heart and life wholly his. God says, "I the Lord have spoken it, and I will do it."

12 The Trial of Faith

But his servants came near and said to him, "My father, if the prophet had commanded you to do some great thing, would you not have done it? How much rather, then, when he says to you, "Wash, and be clean"? (2 Kgs 5:13)

In Naaman we have a striking Old Testament illustration of the place faith takes in God's dealing with man. It reveals what faith really is. Consider how intensely Naaman desired healing. He would do anything—appeal to the king of Syria and the king of Israel, undertake a long journey and humble himself before the prophet, who did not even come out and see him. In this intensity of desire for blessing we have the root of a strong faith. And it is just this seeking for God and his blessing which is too much lacking in Christianity today.

The second mark of faith is that it must give up all its preconceived opinions and bow before the Word of God. This was more than Naaman was willing to do, and he turned away in a rage. It was well for him that a wise and faithful servant gave him better advice. Faith is often held back by the thought of how such a simple thing as accepting God's Word can effect a mighty revolution in the heart.

And then comes the third mark of faith: it submits implicitly to the Word of God. "Wash, and be clean." At first it all seems in vain, but faith proves itself in obedience, and it does it not once or twice but seven times in the assurance that the mighty wonder will be wrought. It takes the simple word, "Wash, and be clean," and finds itself renewed. The mighty deed is done.

When God's Word promises: "I will sprinkle clean water upon you, and you shall be clean from all your uncleannesses," it is nothing but unbelief that holds us back. Let us believe that a simple, determined surrender of the whole will to God's promise will indeed bring the heart-cleansing we need. "There is a river whose streams make glad the city of God." It flows from under the throne of God and the Lamb, through the channels of a thousand precious promises, and at each step the word is heard: "Wash, and be clean." Christ cleanses "by the washing of water with the Word." Every promise is a call: "Wash, and be clean; wash, and be clean"; and Christ will speak: "You are already made clean through the word which I have spoken to you."

13 Faith in Christ
Believe in God, believe also in me. (Jn 14:1)

In the Farewell Discourse (Jn 14-17), when Christ was about to leave his disciples, he taught them to believe in him with the same perfect confidence which they had in God. "Believe in God, believe also in me." "Believe me that I am in the Father." "He who believes in me will also do the works that I do." Here on earth he had not made himself fully known to his disciples. But in heaven, in the fullness of God's power, he would, in and through his disciples, do greater things than he had ever done upon earth. This faith must fix itself first of all on the person of Christ in his union with the Father. All that God had done could now be done by Jesus too. The deity of Christ is the rock on which our faith depends. Christ as man, partaker of our nature, is indeed true God. As the divine power has worked in Christ even to the resurrection from the dead, so Christ can also, in his divine omnipotence, work in us all that we need.

See how important it is that you take time to worship Jesus in his divine omnipotence as one with the Father? This will teach us to count on him in his sufficiency to work in us all that we desire. Faith must so possess us that every thought of Christ will be filled with the consciousness of his presence as an Almighty Redeemer, able to save and sanctify and empower us.

Bow in deep humility before this Lord Jesus, and worship him: my Lord and my God! Come under the full consciousness of an assured faith that as the Almighty God, Christ will work for you and in you and through you all that God desires and all that you can need. Let the Savior you have known and loved become, as never before, the mighty God. Let him be your confidence and your strength.

On the last night, as the Savior was about to leave the world, he told his disciples that through their whole life everything would depend on simply believing him. By that they would even do greater things than he had ever done. And at the close of this discourse he repeated, "Be of good cheer, I have overcome the world." Our one need is a direct, definite, unceasing faith in the mighty power of Christ working in us.

14 Christ's Life in Us
Because I live, you will live also. (Jn 14:19)

There is a great difference in the teaching of the three first Evangelists and that of John. John was the bosom friend of Jesus. He understood the Master better than the others and recorded parts of Christ's teaching about which they say nothing. This makes John 13-17 the inmost sanctuary of the New Testament. The others spoke of repentance and the pardon of sin as the first great gift of the New Testament, but of the new life which the New Covenant was to bring and the new heart in which the law had been put as a living power, they say little. John records what Christ taught about his very own life really becoming ours and about our being united with him just as he was with the Father. The other Evangelists speak of Christ as the Shepherd seeking and saving the lost. John speaks of him as the Shepherd who so gives his life for the sheep, that his very life becomes theirs: "I came that they may have life, and have it abundantly" (Jn 10:10).

The Lord said, "Because I live, you will live also." The

disciples were to receive from him, not the life he then had, but the resurrection life in the power of its victory over death, and the power of his exaltation to the right hand of God. He would then dwell in them; a new, a heavenly, an eternal life, the life of Jesus himself would fill them. This promise is for all who will accept it in faith.

How many there are who are content with the beginnings of the Christian life, but never long to have it in its fullness, the more abundant life! They do not believe in it; they are not ready for the sacrifice implied in being wholly filled with the life of Jesus. The things that are impossible with men are possible with God. Let Christ's wonderful promises possess your heart. Be content with nothing less than a *full* salvation, Christ living in you, and you living in Christ. Be assured that it is meant for everyone who will listen to Christ's promises and believe that the almighty power of God will work in him the mighty wonder of his grace—Christ dwelling in the heart by faith.

15 The Obedience of Love
If you keep my commandments, you will abide in my love. (Jn 15:10)

The question is often asked: How can I abide in Christ? How can I live wholly for him? Such is my desire and fervent prayer. In this text the Lord gives the simple but far-reaching answer: "Keep my commandments." This is the only, the sure, the blessed way of abiding in him. "If you keep my commandments, you will abide in my love, just as I have kept my Father's commandments and abide in his love." Loving obedience is the way to the enjoyment of his love.

Notice how often the Lord speaks of this in the Farewell Discourse. "If you love me, you will keep my commandments" (14:15). And then again twice over: "He who has my commandments and keeps them, he it is who loves me; and he who loves me will be loved of my Father, and I will love him" (14:21). "If a man loves me, he will keep my word; and my Father will love him, and we will come to him and make our home with him" (14:23). And also three times in chapter 15, "If my words abide in you, ask whatever you will, and it shall be done for you" (v. 7); "If you keep my commandments, you will abide in my love" (v. 10); "You are my friends if you do what I command you" (v. 14). Six times over the Lord connects the keeping of the commandments with loving him, and with the promise of the great blessing following on it—the indwelling of the Father and the Son in the heart. Keeping his commandments is the only way to abide in his love. In our whole relation to Christ, love is everything; Christ's love for us, our love for him, proven in our love for others.

How little Christians have accepted this teaching. How content many are with thinking it impossible. They do not believe that through the grace of God we can be kept from sin. They do not believe in the promise of the New Covenant: "I will put my spirit within you, and cause you to walk in my statutes and be careful to observe my ordinances" (Ez 36:27). They have no conception of how Christ alone will make possible to a heart fully surrendered and given over to him alone what otherwise appears beyond our reach: loving him, keeping his commandments, abiding in his love.

The Holy Spirit as the power of Christ's life in the disciples was the pledge that they would indeed love him and keep his words. That was to be the great secret of abiding in Christ, of having the indwelling of Christ and of God, and of the divine efficacy of their prayer to bring down God's blessing on all their work.

16 The Promise of the Spirit
If I do not go away, the Counselor will not come to you; but if I go, I will send him to you. . . . He will glorify me, for he will take what is mine and declare it to you.
(Jn 16:7, 14)

The crucified Christ was to be glorified on the throne of heaven, and out of that glory he would send down the Holy Spirit into the hearts of his disciples to glorify him in them.

The Spirit of the crucified and glorified Christ would be their life in fellowship with him, and their power for his service. The Spirit comes to us as the Spirit of the divine glory; as such we are to welcome him and yield ourselves absolutely to his leading.

The Spirit who searches the deep things of God, who dwells in the very roots of the Divine Being, who was with Christ through all his life and in his death upon the cross, the Spirit of the Father and the Son was to come and dwell in the disciples and make them the conscious possessors of the presence of the glorified Christ. It was this Spirit who was to be their power for a life of loving obedience, their Teacher and Leader in praying down from heaven the blessing that they needed. In his power they were to conquer God's enemies and carry the gospel to the ends of the world.

It is this Spirit of God and of Christ that the Church lacks so sadly; it is this Spirit she grieves so unceasingly. It is owing to this that her work is so often feeble and fruitless. And what can be the reason for this?

The Spirit is God. As God he claims our whole being. We have thought too much of him as our help in the Christian life; we have not known that heart and life are to be entirely and unceasingly under his control. We are to be led by the Spirit every day and every hour. In his power our life is to be a direct and continual abiding in the love and fellowship of Jesus. No wonder we have not believed in the great promise that, in a love that keeps the commandments, we can always abide in Christ's love. No wonder we have not the courage to believe that Christ's mighty power will work in us and through us. No wonder his divine prayer-promises are beyond our reach. The Spirit who searches the deep things of God claims the very depths of our being, there to reveal Christ as Lord and Ruler.

The promise waits for its fulfillment in our life: "He will glorify me, for he will take what is mine and declare it to you." Let us this very day yield ourselves to believe the promise at once and with our whole heart. Christ waits to make it true.

17 In Christ
In that day you will know that I am in my Father, and you in me, and I in you. (Jn 14:20)

Our Lord said of his life in the Father, "Believe me that I am in the Father, and the Father in me." He and the Father were not two persons next each other; they were in each other; though on earth as man, he lived in the Father. All he did was what the Father did in him.

This divine life of heaven, of Christ in God and God in Christ, is the picture and the pledge of what our life in Christ is to be here upon earth. It is in the very nature of the divine life that the Son is in the Father. Even so we must know and ever live in the faith that we are in Christ. Then we will learn that even as the Father worked in Christ, so Christ will also work in us, if we believe that we are in him and yield ourselves to his power.

And even as the Son waited on the Father and the Father worked through him, so the disciples would make known to him in prayer what they wanted done on earth, and he would do it. Their life in him was to be the reflection of his life in the Father. As the Father worked in him, because he lived in the Father, so Christ would work in them as they lived in him.

But this would not be until the Holy Spirit came. They had to wait until they were endued with power from on high. They would abide in him by daily fellowship and prayer until he did in them the greater works he had promised.

How little the Church understands that the secret of her power is to be found in nothing less than where Christ found it, abiding in the Father and his love. How little ministers make this their one great object, daily and hourly to abide in Christ as the only possible way of being equipped and used by him in the great work of winning souls to him. If anyone asks what the lost secret of the pulpit is, we have it here: "In that day"—when the Spirit fills your heart—"you will know that I am in my Father, and you in me."

*Lord, teach us to surrender ourselves unreservedly to the Holy
Spirit; and to daily wait for his teaching, that we too may know
the blessed secret, that as you are in the Father, and the Father
works through you, so we are in you, and you work through us.
Gracious Lord, pour down upon all your children who are seeking
to work for you, such a Spirit of grace and of supplication that we
may not rest until we too are filled with the Holy Spirit.*

18 Abiding in Christ
Abide in me, and I in you. (Jn 15:4)

What our Lord had taught in John 14, concerning union
with him in the likeness of his being in the Father, he
enforces and illustrates by the wonderful parable of the
Branch and the Vine—and all for the sake of bringing home
to the apostles, and to all his servants in the gospel, the
absolute necessity of a life daily in full communion with
him. "Abide in me."

On the one hand he points to himself and to the Father:
Just as truly and fully as I am in the Father, so you are in me.
Then, pointing to the vine: Just as truly as the branch is in
the vine, you are in me. Just as the Father abides in me and
works in me, and I work out what he works in me, and just
as truly as the branch abides in the vine and the vine gives its
life and strength to the branch, and the branch receives it
and puts it forth in fruit—even so do you abide in me and
receive my strength; even so I will work with an almighty
power my work in you and through you. Abide in me!

Perhaps you have often meditated on this passage, but
you realize how much there is still to learn if you are to have
Christ's almighty power working in you as he would wish
you to have. So take time in waiting on the Lord Jesus in the
power of his Spirit, until these two great truths completely
master your being: As Christ is in God, the testimony from
heaven, and as the branch is in the vine, the testimony of all
nature, the law of heaven and the law of earth combine in
calling to us: "Abide in Christ." "He who abides in me,
bears much fruit." Fruit, more fruit, much fruit, is what
Christ seeks, is what he works, is what he will assuredly give
to the one that trusts him.

To the feeblest of God's children Christ says: You are in me. "Abide in me. You shall bear much fruit." To the strongest of his messengers he still has the word—there can be nothing higher: "Abide in me, and you shall bear much fruit." To one and all the message comes: Daily, continuous, unbroken abiding in Christ Jesus is the one condition of a life of power and of blessing. Allow the Holy Spirit to so renew in you the secret abiding in him that you may understand the meaning of his words: "These things have I spoken unto you that my joy might remain in you, and that your joy might be full."

"Do you believe that I can do this, keep you abiding in my love?" "Yes, Lord." "Then fear not, only believe."

19 The Power of Prayer
If you abide in me, and my words abide in you, ask whatever you will, and it shall be done for you. (Jn 15:7)

Before our Lord ascended to heaven he taught his disciples two great lessons in regard to their relation to him in the great work they had to do.

One was that in heaven he would have much more power than he had upon earth, and that he would use that power for the salvation of men—through them, their word, and their work.

The other was that without him they could do nothing, but they could count upon him to work in them and through them and so carry out his purpose. Their first and chief work would therefore be to bring everything they wanted done to him in prayer. In the Farewell Discourse he repeats the promise seven times: "Abide in me, pray in my name"; you can count upon it, "Ask what you will; it shall be done for you."

With these two truths written in their heart, he sent them out into the world. They could confidently undertake their work. The almighty, glorified Jesus was ready to do in and with and through them greater things than he himself had ever done upon earth. The helpless disciples on earth looked unceasingly to him in prayer, fully confident that he would hear that prayer; the first and only condition, an unflinching confidence in the power of his promise. The chief thing in all their life and in the work of their ministry was to maintain a spirit of prayer and supplication.

How little the Church has understood and believed this! And why? Simply because believers live so little in the daily abiding in Christ that they are powerless to believe his great and precious promises. Let us learn, both for our life and our work, that as the members of Christ's body, the chief thing every day must be that close abiding fellowship with Christ, which takes its place of deep dependence and unceasing supplication. Only then can we do our work fully assured that he has heard our prayer and will be faithful in doing his part, giving the power from on high as the source of strength and abundant blessing. Christ asks, "Do you believe this?" "Yes, Lord, I believe." "Abide in me, abide in my love."

"If you abide in me, and my words abide in you, ask whatever you will, and it shall be done for you."

20 The Mystery of Love

I . . . pray . . . that they may all be one; even as thou, Father, art in me, and I in thee, that they may be one even as we are one, I in them and thou in me. (Jn 17:20-23)

In the Farewell Discourse Christ stressed the thought of the disciples being in him and abiding in him. He had also mentioned his being in them, but gave this less prominence than their being in him. But in his prayer as High Priest, he gives larger place to the thought of his being in them, just as the Father was in him. "That they may be one even as we are one; I in them and thou in me, that they may become perfectly one, so that the world may know that thou hast sent me and hast loved them even as thou hast loved me."

The power to convince the world that God loved the disciples as he loved his Son could only come as they lived out the life of having Christ in them, proving it by loving each other as Christ loved them. The feebleness of the Church is due to this—our life in Christ and his life in us is not known and not proved to the world by the living unity in which our love manifests that Christ is in us. Nothing less than this is needed: such an indwelling of Christ in the heart, such a binding together of believers because they know and see and love each other as those who together have Christ dwelling in them. As we have it in the very last words of the prayer, "I made known to them thy name . . . that the love with which thou hast loved me may be in them, and I in them." The divine indwelling has its chief glory in that it is the manifestation of divine love. The Father's love for Christ, brought by Christ to us, flowing out from us to our brothers and sisters and to all men.

Christ promised the loving, obedient disciple, "My Father will love him, and I will love him, and we will come and make our abode with him" (Jn 14:21, 23). It is to live this life of love for Christ and others, that the Holy Spirit, in whom the Father and the Son are one, longs to live in our heart. Let nothing less than this be what you seek, what you believe, what you claim with your whole heart and strength—the indwelling of the Lord Jesus in the "love that surpasses knowledge," with which he can fill your heart. So shall the world indeed be constrained by the love God's children bear to each other to acknowledge that the word is being fulfilled, "that the love with which thou hast loved me may be in them, and I in them."

"Do you believe that I can do this?" "Yes, Lord."

21 Christ Our Righteousness
They are justified by his grace as a gift, through the redemption which is in Christ Jesus. (Rom 3:24)

The first three Evangelists speak of redemption as a pardon of sin, or justification. John speaks of it as a life which Christ is to live in us, or regeneration. In Paul we find both truths in beautiful harmony.

In Romans he first speaks of justification (Rom 3:21-5:11). Then he goes on to speak of the life that there is in union with Christ (5:12-8:39). In Romans 4 he tells us that we find both these things in Abraham. First, "Abraham believed God," "who justifies the ungodly," "his faith is reckoned as righteousness." Then, Abraham believed God, "who gives life to the dead." Just as God first of all counted to Abraham his faith as righteousness, and then led him on to believe in him as the God who can give life to the dead, even so with us.

Justification comes at the commencement full and complete, as the eye of faith is fixed upon Christ. But that is only the beginning. Gradually the Christian begins to understand that he was at the same time born again, that he has Christ *in him*, and that his calling now is to abide in Christ and let Christ abide and live and work in him.

Most Christians strive, by holding fast their faith in justification, to stir and strengthen themselves for a life of gratitude and obedience. But they fail sadly because they do not in full faith yield themselves to Christ who desires to maintain his life in them. They have learned from Abraham the first lesson, to believe in God who justifies the ungodly. But they have not gone on to the second lesson, to believe in God who gives life to the dead and daily renews that life through Christ, who lives in them and in whose life alone there is strength and fullness of blessing. The Christian life must be "from faith to faith." The grace of pardon is but the beginning; growing in grace leads on to the fuller insight and experience of what it is to be *in Christ*, to live in him and to grow up in him in all things as the Head.

22 Christ Our Life
Much more will those who receive the abundance of grace and the free gift of righteousness reign in life through the one man Jesus Christ. (Rom 5:17)
So you also must consider yourselves dead to sin and alive to God in Christ Jesus. (Rom 6:11)

We said that Paul teaches us now that our faith in Christ as our righteousness is to be followed by our faith in him as our life from the dead. He asks, "Do you not know that all of us who have been baptized into Christ Jesus were baptized into his death?" (Rom 6:3). We were buried with him and raised from the dead with him. Just as in Adam all his children died, so all believers in Christ actually died too in him. "Our old man was crucified with him," and with him we were raised from the dead. Now we are to consider ourselves "dead to sin and alive to God."

Indeed, just as the new life in us is an actual participation in and experience of the risen life of Christ, so our death to sin in Christ is also an actual spiritual reality. When we see, by the power of the Holy Spirit, how really we were one with Christ on the cross in his death and in his resurrection, we will understand that in him sin has no power over us. We present ourselves to God "as alive from the dead."

Just as the old Adam lives in the sinner, even in the believer, too, who does not know of the new death in Christ which he has died, even so the man who knows that he died in Christ and now is alive in him can confidently count upon the word, "Sin shall not have dominion over you," not even for a single moment. "Consider yourselves dead to sin and alive to God in Christ Jesus." This is the true life of faith.

As what our Lord said about being in him, and allowing him to live his life in us, could only come true as the full power of the Holy Spirit is experienced, so it is here too. Paul says, "The law of the Spirit of life in Christ Jesus has set me free from the law of sin and death" (Rom 8:2), to which he had felt captive. He then adds that "the just requirement of the law might be fulfilled in us who walk not according to the flesh, but according to the Spirit." Through the Spirit we enter into the glorious liberty of the children of God.

May God open the eyes of his children to see the greatness of the power of Christ living in them for a life of holiness and fruitfulness, when they consider themselves dead unto sin and alive unto God in Christ Jesus.

23 Crucified with Christ
I have been crucified with Christ; it is no longer I who live, but Christ who lives in me. (Gal 2:20)

As in Adam we died to the life and the will of God and fell into sin and corruption, so in Christ we partake of a new spiritual death, a death to sin and so come into the will and the life of God. Such was the death Christ died; such is the death we partake of in him. This was such a reality to Paul that he was able to say, "I have been crucified with Christ; it is no longer I who live, but Christ who lives in me." The death with Christ had had such power that he no longer lived his own life; Christ lived his life in him. He had indeed died to the old nature and to sin, and been raised up into the power of the living Christ dwelling in him.

The crucified Christ lived in him and made him partaker of all that the cross had meant to Christ himself. The very mind that was in Christ—his self-emptying, his taking the form of a servant, his humbling himself to become obedient unto death—these dispositions worked in Paul because the crucified Christ lived in him. He indeed lived as a crucified man.

Christ's death on the cross most highly exhibited his holiness and his victory over sin, and the believer who receives Christ partakes of all the power and blessing that the crucified Lord has won. As the believer learns to accept of this by faith, he yields himself as now crucified to the world and dead to its pleasure and pride, its lusts and self-pleasing. He learns that the mystery of the cross, as the crucified Lord reveals its power in him, opens the entrance into the fullest fellowship with Christ and conformity to his sufferings. And so he learns, in the full depth of its meaning, what the Word has said: "Christ crucified, the power of God and the wisdom of God." He dares to say, "I have been crucified with Christ; it is no longer I who live, but Christ who lives in me."

Oh, the blessedness of the power of the God-given faith that enables a man to live all the day considering himself dead to sin and alive to God in Christ Jesus!

24 The Faith Life
And the life I now live in the flesh I live by faith in the Son of God, who loved me and gave himself for me.
(Gal 2:20)

What did Paul mean when he said that he no longer lived, but that Christ lived in him? Paul himself gives us the answer: "The life I now live in the flesh I live by faith in the Son of God, who loved me and gave himself for me." His whole life, day by day and all the day, was an unceasing faith in the wonderful love that had given itself for him. Faith was the power that possessed and permeated his whole being and his every action.

Here we have the simple but full statement of what the secret of the true Christian life is. It is not faith only in certain promises of God, or in certain blessings that we receive from Christ. It is a faith that has a vision of how entirely Christ gives himself to the soul to be, in the very deepest and fullest sense of the word, his life and all that that implies for every moment of the day. As essential as continuous breathing is to the support of our physical life, so essential is unceasing faith, in which the soul trusts Christ and counts upon him to maintain the life of the Spirit within us. Faith ever rests on that infinite love in which Christ gave himself wholly for us, to be ours in the deepest meaning of the word, and to live his life over again in us. In virtue of his divine omnipresence, whereby he fills all things, he can be to each what he is to all—a complete and perfect Savior, an abiding Guest, taking charge and maintaining our life in us and for us, as if each of us were the only one in whom he lives. Just as truly as the Father lived in him, and worked in him all that he was to work out, just as truly will Christ live and work in each one of us.

Faith, led and taught by God's Holy Spirit, is so confident in the omnipotence and the omnipresence of Christ that it carries in the depth of the heart the abiding unbroken assurance all the day: He who loved me and gave himself for me lives in me; he is indeed my life and my all. "I can do all things through Christ who strengthens me." May God reveal to us that inseparable union between Christ and us in which the consciousness of Christ's presence may become as natural to us as the consciousness of our own existence.

25 Full Consecration
Indeed I count everything as loss because of the surpassing worth of knowing Christ Jesus my Lord.
(Phil 3:8)

In studying the promises Jesus gave to his disciples in the last night, this question arises: What made these men worthy of the high honor of being baptized with the Holy Spirit? The answer is simple. When Christ called them, they forsook all and followed him. They denied themselves, even to the hating of their own life, and gave themselves to obey his commands. They followed him to Calvary, and amid its suffering and death their hearts clung to him alone. This prepared them to receive a share in his resurrection life, and so becoming equipped here on earth to be filled with that Spirit, even as he received the fullness of the Spirit from the Father in glory.

Just as Jesus Christ had to sacrifice all to be wholly an offering to God, so all his people, from Abraham, Jacob, and Joseph down to his twelve apostles, have had to give up everything to follow the divine leading, before the divine power could fulfill his purposes through them.

It was the same with Paul. To count all things as loss for the sake of Christ was the keynote of his life, as it must be that of ours, if we are to share fully in the power of the resurrection. But how little the Church understands that we have been entirely redeemed from the world, to live wholly and only for God and his love. As the merchant who found the treasure in the field had to sell everything he had to purchase it, Christ claims the whole heart and the whole life and the whole strength, if we are to share with him in the victory through the power of the Holy Spirit. The law of the kingdom is unchangeable; count all things as loss for the surpassing worth of knowing Christ Jesus my Lord.

The disciples had to spend years with Christ to be prepared for Pentecost. Christ calls us to walk every day in the closest union with himself, to abide in him without ceasing, and so to live as those who are not their own, but wholly his. It is in this that we will find the path to the fullness of the Spirit.

Let our faith boldly believe that such a life is meant for us. Let our heart's fervent desire be for nothing less than this. Let us love the Lord our God and Christ our Savior with our whole heart, and we will be more than conquerors through him who loved us.

26 Entire Sanctification

May the God of peace himself sanctify you wholly; and may your spirit and soul and body be kept sound and blameless at the coming of our Lord Jesus Christ. He who calls you is faithful, and he will do it. (1 Thes 5:23, 24)

What a promise! One would expect to see all God's children clinging to it, claiming its fulfillment. Unfortunately, unbelief does not know what to think of it, and few count it their treasure and joy.

God is the God of peace—the peace he made by the blood of the cross, the peace that passes all understanding and keeps our hearts and thoughts in Christ Jesus. And this God of peace *himself* promises to sanctify us wholly, in Christ our sanctification, in the sanctification of the Spirit. It is God who is doing the work. None other than he can and will do it. It is in close, personal fellowship with God himself that we become holy.

Should we not rejoice with exceeding joy at this prospect? Yet it is as if the promise is too great. May your spirit—the inmost part of your being, created for fellowship with God—and your soul—the seat of the life and all its powers—and your body, through which sin entered and in which sin proved its power even unto death, but which has been redeemed in Christ—may your spirit, soul, and body be preserved entire, without blame, at the coming of our Lord Jesus Christ.

To prevent our considering this promise too great to be literally true, Paul adds, "He who calls you is faithful, and he will do it." Yes, God has said, "I the Lord have spoken it; and I, in Christ and through the Holy Spirit, will do it." He only asks that we come and abide in close fellowship with himself every day. As the heat of the sun shines on the body and warms it, the fire of his holiness will burn in us and make us holy. Beware of unbelief. It dishonors God and robs your soul of its heritage. Take refuge in the promise: "He who calls you is faithful, and he will do it." Let every thought of your high and holy calling prompt the response: "He who calls you is faithful, and he will do it." Yes, he will do it; and he will give me grace to abide so near him that I might ever be under the cover of his perfect peace and the holiness which he alone can give. *He will do it.*

"All things are possible to him who believes." I believe, Lord; help my unbelief.

27 The Immeasurable Greatness of His Power

I do not cease to give thanks for you, remembering you in my prayers, that the God of our Lord Jesus Christ, the Father of glory, may give you a spirit of wisdom and of revelation in the knowledge of him, having the eyes of your hearts enlightened, that you may know what is the hope to which he has called you, what are the riches of his glorious inheritance in the saints, and what is the immeasurable greatness of his power in us who believe, according to the working of his great might which he accomplished in Christ when he raised him from the dead. (Eph 1:16-20)

Here we have again one of the great texts in regard to which faith has to be exercised—words that will make our faith large and strong and bold. Paul was writing to men who had been sealed with the Holy Spirit, and yet he felt the need of unceasing prayer for the enlightening of the Spirit, that they might know in truth how mighty the power of God was that was working in them. It was nothing less than the very same power, the working of the strength of his might, by which he raised Christ Jesus from the dead.

Christ died on the tree under the weight of the sin of the world and its curse. When he descended into the grave it was under the weight of all that sin and the power of that death which had apparently mastered him. What a mighty working of the power of God, to raise that Man out of the grave to the power and the glory of his throne. By the teaching of the Holy Spirit, we know that that very same power, in the immeasurable greatness of it in those who believe is working in us every day of our life. The One who said to Abraham, "I am God Almighty, nothing is too hard for me," comes to us with the message that what he did, not only in Abraham but in Christ Jesus, is the pledge of what he is doing every moment in our hearts and will do effectively if we learn to trust him.

It is by that Almighty power that the risen and exalted Christ can be revealed in our hearts as our life and our strength. How little believers believe this! Let us trust God for his Holy Spirit to enable us to claim nothing less every day than the immeasurable greatness of this resurrection power working in us.

And let us pray for all believers around us and throughout the Church, that they may have their eyes opened to the wonderful vision of God's almighty resurrection power working in them. And let ministers, like Paul, make this a matter of continual intercession for those among whom they labor. What a difference it would make in their ministry—the unceasing prayer for the Spirit to reveal the power that dwells and works in them.

28 The Indwelling Christ
That Christ may dwell in your heart through faith.
(Eph 3:17; see also Eph 3:14-16, 18-19)

The great privilege that separated Israel from other nations was this: they had God dwelling in their midst, his home in the holiest of all, in the tabernacle and the temple. The New Testament is the dispensation of the indwelling God in the heart of his people. As Christ said, "He who has my commandments and keeps them, he it is who loves me; ... and my Father will love him, and we will come to him and make our home with him" (Jn 14:21, 23). Paul calls this "the riches of the glory of this mystery among the Gentiles, which is Christ in you, the hope of glory." Or, as he says of himself, "Christ lives in me."

The gospel—the dispensation of the indwelling Christ. How few Christians there are who believe or experience it! Consider Paul's teaching concerning the way to experience this crowning blessing of the Christian life.

1. "I bow my knees before the Father, ... that he may grant you. . . ." The blessing must come from the Father to the supplicant on the bended knee, for himself or for those

for whom he labors. It is to be found in much prayer.

2. "That according to the riches of his glory he may grant you"—something very special and divine—"to be strengthened with might through his Spirit in the inner man," to die to sin and the world, to yield to Christ as Lord and Master, and to live that life of love for Christ and keeping his commandments to which has been promised: "The Father and I will come to him, and make our home with him."

3. "... that Christ may dwell in your heart through faith." It is in the very nature of Christ, in his divine omnipresence and love, to long for the heart to dwell in. As faith sees this and bows the knee, and pleads with God for this great blessing, it receives grace to believe that the prayer is answered; and in that faith accepts the wonderful gift so long thirsted for—Christ dwelling in the heart by faith.

4. "... that you, being rooted and grounded in love, may be filled with all the fullness of God," as far as it is possible for man to experience it.

With strong desire and childlike faith, meditate on these words, on what the Father, and the Son, and the Holy Spirit have undertaken to work in you. Hold fast the confident assurance that God will do abundantly above what we can ask or think.

Christ speaks to you: "According unto your faith be it unto you."

29 Christian Perfection

Now may the God of peace . . . equip you with everything good that you may do his will, working in you that which is pleasing in his sight, through Jesus Christ. (Heb 13:20, 21)

Prepare your heart for a large and strong faith, here again to take in one of those promises of God, as high above all our thoughts as the heaven is above the earth.

What a wonderful exposition we have in the epistle to the Hebrews of that eternal redemption which Christ our great High Priest, the mediator of the New Covenant, worked out for us through the shedding of his blood. The writer closes his whole argument, and all its deep spiritual teaching with this benediction: "May the God of peace equip you with everything good that you may do his will." Does that not include everything? Can we desire more? Yes—"working in you that which is pleasing in his sight, through Jesus Christ."

All that Christ had wrought out for our redemption, and all that God did in raising him from the dead, was done to enable him to work out in us that everlasting redemption. God the Omnipotent will equip us to do his will—he himself will perfect us. And if we want to know how, we have the answer: By working within us that which is pleasing in his sight. And that through Jesus Christ.

All that we have been taught about the completeness of the salvation in Christ, and our call to look on him, to follow him, is here crowned and finds its consummation in the assurance that God himself takes entire charge of the man who really trusts him and through Jesus Christ works all that is pleasing in his sight.

The thought is too high, the promise is too large; we cannot comprehend it. And yet there it is, claiming, stimulating our faith. It calls us to take hold of the one truth—the everlasting God works in me every hour of the day through Jesus Christ. I have just one thing to do, to yield myself into God's hands for him to work, to not hinder him by my working, but in a silent adoring faith to be assured that he himself through Jesus Christ will work in me all that is pleasing in his sight. "Lord, increase our faith!"

30 The God of All Grace
And after you have suffered a little while, the God of all grace, who has called you to his eternal glory in Christ, will himself restore, establish, and strengthen you. (1 Pt 5:10)

We know how the epistle to the Hebrews gathers up all its teaching in that wonderful promise, "May the God of peace equip you that you may do his will." Peter does the same thing here: "The God of all grace will himself restore, establish, and strengthen you." God himself is to be the one object of our trust, day by day; as we think of our work, of our needs, of our life and all our heart's desire, God himself must be the one object of our hope and trust.

Just as God is the center of the universe, the one source of its strength, the one Guide who orders and controls its movements, so God must have the same place in the life of the believer. With every new day the first and chief thought should be—God, God alone, can equip me this day to live as he would have me.

And what is now to be our position towards this God? Should not the first thought of every day be the humble placing of ourselves in his hands to confess our absolute helplessness, yielding ourselves in childlike surrender to receive from him the fulfillment of such promises as these: "May the God of peace equip you to do his will"; "The God of all grace will himself restore, establish, and strengthen you"?

How absolutely indispensable it is to meet God every morning and give him time to reveal himself and to take charge of our life for the day. Is this not what we must do with these words of Peter?

Heavenly Father, in view of the life and work of this new day, my heart is resting on you; my hope is in your Word: "May the God of peace equip you to do his will"; "The God of all grace will himself restore, establish, and strengthen you."

By your grace, may this be the spirit in which I awake every morning to go out to my work, humbly trusting that you will perfect me. You will perfect all that concerns me.

Father, open our eyes to see that even as your Son was perfected forever, so you wait to perfect your saints, that your glory might be seen.

Month Five

1 Not Sinning
You know that he appeared to take away sins, and in him there is no sin. No one who abides in him sins.
(1 Jn 3:5, 6)

John had taken deep into his heart and life the words that Christ had spoken about abiding in him. He remembered how the Lord had six times over spoken of loving him and keeping his commandments as the way to abiding in his love and receiving the indwelling of the Father and the Son. And so in his old age the abiding in Christ is one of the key-words of the life his epistle promises (1 Jn 2:6, 24, 28; 3:6, 24; 4:13, 16).

In our text John teaches how we can be kept from sinning: "No one who abides in him sins." Though there be sin in our nature, the abiding in Christ, in whom is no sin, frees us from the power of sin and enables us to live lives pleasing to God. Jesus said, "I do always those things that please him" (Jn 8:29). And John writes, "Beloved, if our hearts do not condemn us, we have confidence before God; and we receive from him whatever we ask, because we keep his commandments and do what pleases him."

Let the soul that longs to be free from the power of sin take to heart these simple but far-reaching words: "In him is no sin," and "of God I am in him." "He that establishes us in Christ is God." As I seek to abide in him in Whom there is no sin, he will live out his own sinless life in me in the power of the Holy Spirit, and equip me for a life in which I always do the things that are pleasing in his sight.

You are called to a life in which faith, great faith, strong faith, continuous and unbroken faith, in the almighty power of God is your one hope. As you day by day take time and yield yourself to the God of peace, who equips you to do his will, you will experience that what the heart has not conceived is what God indeed works in those who wait for him.

"No one who abides in him sins." The promise is sure: God the almighty is pledged that he will work in you what is pleasing in his sight, through Christ Jesus. In that faith, abide in him.

"No one who abides in him sins."

"Did I not tell you that if you would believe you would see the glory of God?"

2 Overcoming the World
Who is it that overcomes the world but he who believes that Jesus is the Son of God? (1 Jn 5:5)

Christ spoke strongly on the world's hatred of him. His kingdom and the kingdom of this world were in deadly hostility. John understood this and summed it up in these words: "We know that we are of God, and the whole world is in the power of the evil one" (1 Jn 5:19). "Do not love the world or the things in the world. If any one loves the world, love for the Father is not in him" (1 Jn 2:15).

John also teaches us what the real nature and power of the world is: the lust of the flesh, with its self-pleasing; the lust of the eyes, with its seeing and seeking the glory of the world; and the pride of life, with its self-exaltation. We find these three marks of the world in Eve in paradise. She "saw that the tree was good for food, and that it was a delight to the eyes, and the tree was to be desired to make one wise." Through the body, and the eyes, and the pride of wisdom, the world acquired the mastery over her and over us.

The world still exerts a terrible influence over the Christian who does not know that in Christ he has been crucified to the world. In the pleasure in eating and drinking, in the love and enjoyment of its glory, and in all that constitutes the pride of life, the power of this world proves itself. And most Christians are either utterly ignorant of the danger of a worldly spirit, or feel themselves utterly impotent to conquer it.

Christ left us with the great far-reaching promise: "Be of good cheer, I have overcome the world." As the child of God abides in Christ and seeks to live the heavenly life in the power of the Holy Spirit, he may confidently count on the power to overcome the world. "Who is it that overcomes the world but he who believes that Jesus is the Son of God?" "I live by the faith of the Son of God, who loved me, and gave himself for me"; this is the secret of daily, hourly victory over the world and all its secret, subtle temptation. But it requires a heart and a life entirely possessed by the faith of Jesus Christ to maintain the victor's attitude at all times. Ask yourself whether you believe with your whole heart in the victory that faith gives over the world. Put your trust in the mighty power of God, and in the abiding presence of Jesus, as the only pledge of certain and continual victory.

"Do you believe this?" Yes, Lord, I believe.

3 Jesus the Author and Perfecter of Our Faith
I believe; help my unbelief! (Mk 9:24)

What a treasure of encouragement these words contain. Our Lord said to the father of the possessed child, who had asked for his help: "All things are possible to him who believes." The father felt that Christ was throwing the responsibility on him. If he believed, the child could be healed. And he felt as if he had not such faith. But as he looked in the face of Christ, he felt assured that the love which was willing to heal would also be ready to help with his faith and graciously accept even its feeble beginnings. So he cried out, "I believe; help my unbelief!" Christ heard the prayer, and the child was healed.

How often have we felt, as we listened to the wonderful promises of God, that our faith was too feeble to grasp the precious gift. Yet here we are assured that the Christ who waits for our faith to do its work is a Savior who himself will care for our faith. Let us come, however feeble our faith may be, and cry out, "I believe; help my unbelief!" Christ will accept the prayer that puts its trust in him. Exercise your faith, even though it be but as a mustard seed; in contact with Christ the feeblest faith is made strong and bold. Jesus Christ is the author and perfecter of our faith.

As you read God's wonderful promises and long to have them fulfilled, remember the grain of mustard seed. However small, if it is put into the ground and allowed to grow, it becomes a great tree. Take the hidden feeble seed of the little faith you have, with the Word of promise on which you are resting, and plant it in your heart. Confess it in fervent prayer to Christ. He will accept the feeble, trembling faith that clings to him and will not let him go. A feeble faith in an almighty Christ will become the great faith that can move mountains.

We saw in Abraham how God took charge of his faith and trained him to become strong in faith, giving glory to God. Count most confidently on the desire of Christ to strengthen your faith. When he asks, "Do you believe that I can do this?" confidently say, "Yes, Lord, I do believe." Praise God! I have a Christ who not only waits to give us the heavenly life and the blessings of the covenant, but a Christ who secretly works in us the faith that can claim it all.

4 The Lost Secret
Wait for the promise of the Father. . . . You shall be baptized with the Holy Spirit. (Acts 1:4, 5)

After our Lord commanded the disciples, "Go into all the world and preach the gospel to the whole creation," he added another, his very last, command: "Wait for the promise of the Father." "Before many days you shall be baptized with the Holy Spirit."

All Christians agree that the great command to preach the gospel to the whole creation was not only for the disciples, but is binding on us too. But all do not appear to consider the very last command—not to preach until they had received the power from on high—is equally as binding on us as it was on the disciples. The Church appears to have lost possession of that which ought to be to her a secret of secrets—the abiding consciousness, day by day, that it is only as she lives in the power of the Holy Spirit that she can preach the gospel in demonstration of the Spirit and of power. It is owing to this that there is so much preaching and working with so little of spiritual result. It is owing to nothing but this that there is so little prayer, and especially so little of that much-availing prayer that brings down the power from on high on her ministrations.

Let us study the secret of Pentecost as found in the words and the deeds of our Master, and in the words and the deeds of his disciples as they took him at his word. They continued with one accord in prayer and supplication, until the promise was fulfilled, and they were filled with the Holy Spirit, and proved what the mighty power of their God could do through them.

Let us earnestly seek the grace of the Holy Spirit, who alone can himself reveal to us what eye has not seen, nor ear heard, nor entered into the heart of man to conceive—the things which God has done and loves to do for those who wait upon him. Pray that the lost secret may be found—the sure promise that in answer to fervent prayer the power of the Holy Spirit will indeed be given.

5 The Kingdom of God
To them he presented himself alive after his passion by many proofs, appearing to them during forty days, and speaking of the kingdom of God. (Acts 1:3)

When Christ began to preach he took up the message of John: "The kingdom of heaven is at hand." Later on he said, "There are some standing here who will not taste death before they see that the kingdom of God has come with power." That could not be until the King had ascended his throne. Then they would receive from the Father the great gift of the Holy Spirit, bringing down the kingdom of God in its heavenly power into their hearts.

Our text tells us that all the teaching of Jesus, during the forty days after the resurrection, dealt with the kingdom of God. Luke, in the last verses of Acts, sums up all the teaching of Paul at Rome; he testified to the kingdom of God, he preached the kingdom of God (Acts 28:23, 31).

Christ seated upon the throne of God is King and Lord of all. To his disciples he entrusted the announcement of the kingdom, which is righteousness and peace and joy in the Holy Spirit. After he ascended his throne, the prayer he taught them, "Our Father, who art in heaven, thy kingdom come," had for them a new meaning. The rule of God as seen in heaven came down in the power of the Spirit, and the disciples were full of one thought—to preach the coming of the Spirit into the hearts of men. There was now on earth good tidings of the kingdom of God, ruling and dwelling with men, even as in heaven.

In the last command our Lord gave to his disciples (Acts 1:4, 8) we shall find the great essential characteristics of the kingdom put in great power.

1. The King: the crucified Christ. 2. The disciples: his faithful followers. 3. The power for their service: the Holy Spirit. 4. Their work: testifying for Christ as his witnesses. 5. Their aim: the ends of the earth. 6. Their first duty: waiting on God in united unceasing prayer.

If we are to take up and continue the prayer of the disciples, we must have a clear and full impression of all that Christ spoke to them in that last moment, and what it meant for their inner life and all their service.

6 Christ As King

And he said to them, "Truly, I say to you, there are some standing here who will not taste death before they see that the kingdom of God has come with power. (Mk 9:1)

The first mark of the Church: *Christ as King.*

Christ and John the Baptist both preached that the kingdom of God was at hand. In our text Christ said that within the lifetime of some who heard him the kingdom would come in power. That could mean nothing else but that when he, as King, had ascended the throne of the Father, the kingdom would be revealed in the hearts of his disciples by the power of the Holy Spirit. In the kingdom of heaven, God's will was always being done; in the power of the Holy Spirit, Christ's disciples would do his will even as it was done in heaven.

The mark of what a kingdom is, is to be seen in *the king*. Christ now reigns as God and Man on the throne of the Father. On earth there is no embodiment or external manifestation of the kingdom; its power is seen in the lives of those in whom it rules. It is only in the Church, the members of Christ, that the united body can be seen and known. Christ lives and dwells and rules in their hearts. Our Lord himself taught how close the relationship would be. "In that day you will know that I am in my Father, and you in me, and I in you." Next to the faith of his oneness with God, and his omnipotent power, would be the knowledge that they lived in him and he in them.

If we are to follow in the steps of the disciples and share their blessing, we, too, must know that Christ dwells and rules in our hearts *as King*. We live in him, and in his power we are able to accomplish all that he would have us do. Our whole life is to be devoted to our King and the service of his kingdom.

This relationship to Christ will mean, above all, a daily fellowship with him in prayer. The prayer life is to be a continuous and unbroken exercise. In that way his people can rejoice in their King, and in him can be more than conquerors.

7 Jesus the Crucified
God has made him both Lord and Christ, this Jesus whom you crucified. (Acts 2:36)

We have spoken of Christ as King in more than one respect. But we must remember that this King is none other than the *crucified* Jesus. All that we have to say of him, his divine power, his abiding presence, his wonderful love, does not teach us to know him aright unless we maintain the deep consciousness that our King is the crucified Jesus. God has placed him in the midst of his throne as a Lamb that has been slain, and it is thus that the hosts of heaven adore him.

It is thus that we worship him as a King.

Christ's cross is his highest glory. It is through his cross that he has conquered every enemy and gained his place on the throne of God. And it is through his cross that he will impart to us too the knowledge of what the victory over sin is to mean. When Paul wrote, "I have been crucified with Christ, Christ lives in me," he taught us that it was as the Crucified One that Christ ruled on the throne of his heart, and that the spirit of the cross would triumph in us as it did in him.

This was true of the disciples. It prepared them to receive the Holy Spirit. They had, with their Lord, been crucified to the world. The old man had been crucified; in their Lord they were dead to sin and their life was hid with Christ in God. Each one of us needs to experience this fellowship with Christ in his cross if the Spirit of Pentecost is to possess us. It was through the Eternal Spirit that Christ gave himself a sacrifice and became the King on the throne of God. It is as we become "comfortable to his death," in the entire surrender of our will, in the entire self-denial of our old nature, in the entire separation from the spirit of this world, that we can become the worthy servants of a crucified King and our hearts the worthy temples of his glory.

8 The Apostles
And while staying with them he charged them not to depart from Jerusalem, but to wait for the promise of the Father. (Acts 1:4)

The second mark of the Church is to be found in *the disciples* whom the Lord had prepared to receive his Spirit and to be his witnesses. If we would understand the outpouring of the Spirit in answer to the prayer of the disciples, we must above all ask: What was there in these men that equipped them for such powerful, effectual prayer and the wonderful fulfillment of the promise that came to them? They were simple, unlearned men with many faults, whom the Lord had called to forsake all and follow him. They had done this, as far as they could; they followed him in the life he led and the work he did. Though there was much sin in them and they had as yet no power fully to deny themselves, their hearts clung to him in deep sincerity. In the midst of much stumbling they yet followed him. They shared with him his death; unconsciously, but most really, they died with him to sin and were raised with him in the power of a new life. It was this that enabled them to receive the power in prayer and to be clothed with power from on high.

Let this be the test by which we try ourselves: have we indeed surrendered to the fellowship of Christ's sufferings and death? Have we hated our own life and crucified it, and received the power of Christ's life in us? This will free us to believe that God will hear our prayer too, and give us his Holy Spirit to work in us what we and he desire, if we are indeed with one accord to take up the disciples' prayer and to share in the answer. We must, like them, be willing learners in the school of Jesus, and seek above all else that intimate fellowship with him, which will enable us to pray the prayer of Pentecost and receive its answer.

9 Not of This World
They are not of the world, even as I am not of the world.
(Jn 17:14, 16)

In the last night our Lord took pains to make clear to his disciples the impassable gulf between him and the world, and between them and the world (Jn 16:16-21). He had said that the world cannot receive the Spirit of truth, "because it neither sees him nor knows him." "Because you are not of the world . . . therefore the world hates you."

One great mark of the disciples was thus to be as little of the world as Christ was. Christ and they had become united in the cross and the resurrection; they both belonged to another world, the kingdom of heaven. This separation from the world is to be the mark of all disciples who long to be filled with the Spirit.

Why is faith in the Holy Spirit so little preached and practiced? The world rules too much in the life of Christians. Christians live too little the heavenly life to which they are called in Christ Jesus. The "love of the world"; "the lust of the flesh" (pleasure in eating and drinking, in ease and comfort); "the lust of the eyes" (delight in all that the world offers of beauty and possession); the vain glory of life (the self-exaltation in what the wisdom and power of man has accomplished)—all this robs the heart of its desire for that true self-denial that enables it to receive the Holy Spirit.

Let each one who would take up the pentecostal prayer for the power of the Holy Spirit examine himself. Is the spirit of the world the secret of that lack of love of prayer which is absolutely necessary in all who would plead the promise of the Father? May the Lord write this deep in every heart: the world cannot receive the Holy Spirit! "You are not of the world, even as I am not of the world."

10 Obedience

If you love me, you will keep my commandments. And I will pray the Father, and he will give you another Counselor. (Jn 14:15, 16)

We have learned to know the disciples in their training for the baptism of the Spirit, and seen what was needed for their continuing "with one accord" in the prayer for the power of the Spirit. Christ was everything to them, even before the cross, but much more after it. With the resurrection, he was literally their life, their one thought, their only desire.

Such a devotion to Christ—was this something special and not to be expected of all? Or was it indeed something that the Lord asked from all who desire to be filled with the Spirit? Yes, God expects it of all his children; the Lord has need of such now, as much as then, to receive his Spirit and his power, to use them here on earth, and, as intercessors, to link the world to the throne of God.

Is Christ something, or nothing, or everything to us? For the unconverted, Christ is nothing; for the half converted—the average Christian—Christ is something; for the true Christian, Christ is all. Each one who prays for the power of the Spirit must be ready to say: "I yield myself with my whole heart this day to the leading of the Spirit"; a full surrender is an absolute necessity.

"If you love me, keep my commandments." The surrender to live every day, all the day, abiding in Christ and keeping his commandments, is to be the one mark of your discipleship. It is when the child of God learns that it is only as the heart longs in everything to do God's will, that the Father's love and Spirit can rest upon it. This was the disposition in which the disciples continued with one accord in prayer. This will be the secret of power in our intercession as we plead for the Church and the world.

11 The Holy Spirit
You shall be baptized with the Holy Spirit. . . . You shall receive power when the Holy Spirit has come upon you. (Acts 1:5, 8)

The third mark of the Church: *the power for service through the Holy Spirit.* Since the time of Adam's fall, God's Spirit had striven with men and worked in some with power, but he had never been able to find his permanent home in them.

It was only when Christ had come and by his death broken the power of sin, winning in the resurrection a new life for men to live in himself, that the Spirit of God could come and possess the whole heart, and make it a dwelling place for Christ and for God.

Nothing less than this could empower the disciples and us to overcome sin, "setting the prisoners free." This Spirit is the Holy Spirit. In the Old Testament he was called the Spirit of God. Now that in the cross of Christ the holiness of God has been magnified and we may be sanctified like him, the Spirit of God's holiness descends to dwell in men, possessing them as God's holy temple.

He is the Spirit of the Son. On earth he led the Son first into the desert to be tempted of Satan, then to the synagogue in Nazareth to proclaim himself as the fulfillment of what the prophets had spoken (Is 61:1; Lk 4:18). And even on the cross, Christ yielded himself to the leading of the Spirit.

That Spirit now reveals Christ in us as, first of all, our life, and then our strength for a perfect obedience and for the preaching of the Word in the power of God.

Amazing mystery! The Spirit of God, our life; the Spirit of Christ, our light and strength. It is as men and women who are led by this Spirit that we, like the first disciples, will have the power to pray the effectual prayer, the prayer of the righteous man that avails much.

12 The Power from on High
Stay in the city, until you are clothed with power from on high. (Lk 24:49)

The Lord had said to the disciples: "Apart from me you can do nothing." Why did he choose to send out these impotent, helpless men to conquer the world for him? It was that in their feebleness they might yield themselves and give him, as Lord, the opportunity on his throne to show his power working through them. As the Father had done all the work in Christ when he was upon earth, so Christ in heaven would now be the Great Worker, proving in them that all power had been given to him in heaven and on earth. Their place would be to pray, to believe, and yield themselves to the mighty power of Christ.

The Holy Spirit would not be in them as a power which they could possess. Rather, he would possess them, and their work would indeed be the work of the almighty Christ. Their whole posture each day would be that of unceasing dependence and prayer, and of confident expectation.

The apostles learned to know Christ intimately. They had seen all his mighty works; they had received his teaching; they had gone with him through all his sufferings, even to the death of the cross. And they had not only seen him but known him in the power of his resurrection and the experience of that resurrection life in their own hearts. Yet they were not capable of making him known until he himself, from the throne of heaven, had taken possession of them by his Spirit dwelling in them.

Be content with nothing less than the indwelling life and power of the Holy Spirit revealing Jesus in the heart. Only this equips us to preach the gospel in power. Nothing less than having Christ speaking through us in the power of his omnipotence will make us able ministers of the New Testament, bringing salvation to those who hear us.

13 My Witnesses
You shall be my witnesses. (Acts 1:8)

The fourth mark of Christ's Church: *his servants are to be witnesses to him,* ever testifying of his wonderful love, his power to redeem, his continual abiding presence, and his power to work in them.

This is the only weapon that the King allows his redeemed ones to use. Without claiming authority or power, without wisdom or eloquence, without influence or position, each one is called, not only by his words but by his life and action, to be a living proof and witness of what Jesus can do.

This is to be the only weapon they are to use in conquering men and bringing them to the feet of Christ. This is what the first disciples did. When they were filled with the Spirit they began to speak of the mighty things that Christ had done.

It was in this power that those who were scattered abroad by persecution went forth, even as far as Antioch, preaching in the name of Jesus, so that a multitude believed. They had no commission from the apostles; they had no special gifts or training; but out of the fullness of the heart they spoke of Jesus Christ. They could not be silent; they were filled with the life and the love of Christ, and could not but witness to him.

It was this that gave the gospel its power of increase; every new convert became a witness for Christ.

A non-Christian writer tells later in regard to the persecutions, that if the Christians were only content to keep the worship of Jesus to themselves they would not have to suffer. But in their zeal they wanted Christ to rule over all.

Here we have the secret of a flourishing Church: every believer a witness for Jesus. Here we have the cause of the weakness of the Church: so few who are willing in daily life to testify that Jesus is Lord.

What a call to prayer! Lord, teach your disciples to so know Jesus and the power of his love, that they find their highest joy in witnessing to what he is and has done for them.

14 The Gospel Ministry
The Spirit of truth . . . will bear witness to me; and you also are witnesses, because you have been with me from the beginning. (Jn 15:26, 27)

My "witnesses"—that not only refers to all believers, but very especially to all ministers of the gospel. This is the high calling and also the only power of the preacher of the gospel—in everything to be a witness for Jesus.

This gives us two great truths. The first is that with all that the preacher teaches from the Word of God, or according to the need of his congregation, he must place the preaching of Christ himself first. This is what the first disciples did. "They ceased not in every house to teach and to preach Jesus Christ." This was what Philip did at Samaria. "He preached Christ to them." And so Paul writes: "I determined not to know anything among you, save Jesus Christ and him crucified."

The minister of the gospel may never forget that it is especially for this that he has been set apart, to be with the Holy Spirit a witness for Christ. It is as he does this that sinners will find salvation, that God's children will be sanctified and equipped for his service. Only in this way can Christ have his place in the heart of his people and in the world around.

But there is a second thought of no less importance: the teaching must ever be a personal testimony from experience to what Christ is and can do. As this note is sounded, the Holy Spirit carries the message as a living reality to the heart. It is this that will build up believers so that they can walk in such fellowship with Jesus Christ that he can reveal himself through them. And it is this that will lead them to the knowledge of the indispensable secret of spiritual health—the prayer life in daily fellowship, in childlike love, and true consecration with the Father and the Son.

What abundant matter for united prayer, to cultivate among believers and ministers that joy of the Holy Spirit in which, out of the abundance of the heart, the mouth speaks to the praise and glory of our Redeemer, Jesus Christ our Lord.

15 To the End of the Earth
My witnesses . . . to the end of the earth. (Acts 1:8)

Here we have the fifth mark of Christ's Church: his disciples are to be his witnesses *to the end of the earth*.

What words are these for the man who in his absolute impotence had been crucified by his enemies, speaking of the end of the earth as his dominion. What folly on the part of those who speak of Christ as being nothing but a man. How could it have entered the mind of any writer to venture the prophecy that a Jew who had been crucified, whose whole life had been proved by that cross to be an utter failure, and whose disciples had at the last utterly forsaken him—that by them he should conquer the world? No human mind could have formed such a conception. It is the thought of God; he alone could plan and execute such a purpose.

The word that Jesus spoke to his disciples, "You shall receive power when the Holy Spirit has come upon you," assured them that the Holy Spirit would maintain in them Christ's divine power. As Christ did his works only because the Father worked in him, so Christ assured his disciples that he himself from the throne of heaven would work all their works in them. They could ask what they would and it would be done for them. In the strength of that promise the Church of Christ can make the end of the earth its one aim.

The extension of God's kingdom can only be effected by the united, continued prayer of men and women who give their hearts wholly to wait upon Christ assured that what they desire he will do for them.

May God grant that his children would prove their faith in Christ by making his aim their aim and yielding themselves to be his witnesses in united, persevering prayer, waiting upon him fully assured that he will most gloriously give all that they ask.

Become one of those intercessors who really believe that in answer to your prayer the crucified Jesus will do far more than you can ask or think.

16 The Whole Earth Filled with His Glory
Blessed be his glorious name for ever; may his glory fill the whole earth! Amen and Amen! (Ps 72:19)

What a prospect! This earth now under the power of the Evil One, renewed and filled with the glory of God—a new earth in which righteousness dwells. Though we believe it so little, it will surely come to pass; God's Word is the pledge of it. God's Son by his blood and death conquered the power of sin, and through the eternal Spirit the power of God is working out his purpose. What a vision, the whole earth filled with his glory!

But what a great and difficult work. It is near two thousand years since Christ gave the promise and ascended the throne, and yet more than one-half of the human race have never learned to know even the name of Jesus. And of the other half, millions who are called by his name still know him not. This great work of bringing the knowledge of Christ to every creature has been entrusted to a Church that thinks little of her responsibility and of what the consequence of her neglect will be. We may indeed ask: Will the work ever be done? His power and his faithfulness are pledges that one day we shall see the whole earth filled with the glory of God.

What a wonderful prayer! For in our text it is a prayer—"May his glory fill the whole earth! Amen and Amen!" It is to this prayer that every believer is called, and he can count upon the Holy Spirit to inspire and to strengthen him. We desire to strengthen each other, so that every day of our life, with all the power there is in us, we with one accord and continually desire to pray this in the name of Jesus and the power of his Spirit.

True prayer will indeed help, and be answered! How good it is to every day of our lives seek God's face, with confidence to lay hold of him and give him no rest until the earth is full of his glory! How good it is to unite with all God's willing children who are seeking to prepare the way for our King in this, the day of his power.

17 The First Prayer Meeting
All these with one accord devoted themselves to prayer, together with the women. (Acts 1:14)

The sixth mark of the early Church: *waiting on the promise of the Father in united prayer.*

It is difficult to conceive of the unspeakable importance of this first prayer meeting in the history of the kingdom, a prayer meeting which was the simple fulfilling of the command of Christ. It was to indicate for all time the one condition on which his presence and Spirit would be known in power. In it we have the key that opens the storehouse of heaven with all its blessings.

Christ had prayed that the disciples might be one, even as he and the Father were one, that the world might know that God loved them as he loved Christ. How far the disciples were from such a state when Christ prayed the prayer, we see in the strife that there was among them at the Lord's Table concerning which one was the greatest. Only after the resurrection and ascension would they be brought, in the ten days of united supplication, to that holy unity of love and of purpose which would make them the one body of Christ prepared to receive the Spirit in all his power.

What a prayer meeting—the fruit of Christ's training during his three years with them. Adam's body was first created, before God breathed his Spirit into him, and so the body of Christ had first to be formed before the Spirit took possession.

This prayer meeting gives us the law of the kingdom for all time. Where Christ's disciples are linked to each other in love and yield themselves wholly to him in undivided consecration, the Spirit will be given from heaven as the seal of God's approval and Christ will show his mighty power. One of the great marks of the new dispensation is the united unceasing prayer that avails much and is crowned with the power of the Holy Spirit. Is this not why, if our prayers are confined in great measure to our own church or interests, the answer cannot come in such power as we expected?

18 The Unity of the Spirit
Eager to maintain the unity of the Spirit. . . . There is one body and one Spirit. (Eph 4:3, 4)

From Paul we learn how the Christian communities in different places ought to remember each other in the fellowship of prayer. He points out how in such prayer God is glorified and writes more than once (2 Cor 1:11; 4:15; 9:12, 13) of how the ministry of intercession abounds to the glory of God.

The children of God throughout the world need to be drawn close together in the consciousness of being chosen by God to be a holy priesthood, ministering continually the sacrifice of praise and prayer. There is too little distinction between the world and the body of Christ; in the life of many of God's children there is very little difference from what the world is. It is a question of the deepest importance: What can be done to foster the unity of the Spirit?

Nothing will help so much as a life of more prayer, interceding that God's people may prove their unity in a life of holiness and love. That will be a living testimony to the world of what it means to live for God. When Paul wrote, "Pray at all times in the Spirit, with all prayer and supplication. To that end, keep alert with all perseverance, making supplication for all the saints," he names one of the essential characteristics of the difference between God's people and the world.

You may long to bear this mark of the children of God and prove to yourself and to others that you are indeed not of the world. Resolve in your life to bear this one great distinctive feature of the true Christian—a life of prayer and intercession. Join with God's children who are seeking with one accord and unceasingly to maintain the unity of the Spirit and the body of Christ, that they may be strong in the Lord and in the power of his might and to pray down a blessing upon his Church. Let none of us consider too much to give a quarter of an hour every day for meditation on some word of God connected with his promises to his Church and then to plead with him for its fulfillment. Slowly, unobservedly, and yet surely, you will taste the goodness of being one, heart and soul, with God's people and receive the power to pray the effectual prayer that avails much.

19 Union Is Strength

And when they had prayed, . . . and they were all filled with the Holy Spirit and spoke the word of God with boldness. Now the company of those who believed were of one heart and soul. (Acts 4:31, 32)

The power of union we see everywhere in nature. How feeble is a drop of rain as it falls to earth, but when the many drops are united in one stream, and thus become one body, how quickly the power becomes irresistible. Such is the power of true union in prayer. In Psalm 34:5 the English margin has, instead of "They looked unto Him," "They flowed unto Him." The Dutch translation is, "They rushed towards Him like a stream of water." Such was the prayer in the upper room. And such can our prayer be if we unite all our forces in pleading the promise of the Father. And when the world "comes in like a flood," it can be overcome in the power of united prayer.

In Natal, owing to the many mountains, the streams often flow down with great force. The Zulus are accustomed, when they wish to pass through a stream, to join hands. The leader has a strong stick in the right hand, and gives his left hand to some strong man who comes behind him. And so they form a chain of twelve or twenty, and help each other to stem and cross the current. Let us believe that when in spirit God's people reach out their hands to each other, there will be power to resist the terrible influence that the world can exert. And in that unity God's children, when they have overcome the power of the world and the flesh, will have power to prevail with God.

It was in the upper room that they waited ten days until they had truly become one heart and one soul. When the

Spirit of God descended, he not only filled each individual, but took possession of the whole company as the body of Christ.

In this twentieth century the prayer of our Lord Jesus is still being offered: "Father, that they may be one as we are one." It is in the fellowship of loving and believing prayer that our hearts can be melted into one, and that we shall become strong in faith to believe and to accept what God has promised us.

20 Prayer in the Name of Christ
Whatever you ask in my name, I will do it, that the Father may be glorified in the Son. (Jn 14:13)

How wonderful the link between our prayers and Christ's glorifying the Father in heaven. Much prayer on earth brings him much glory in heaven. What an incentive to prayer, to unceasing intercession. Our prayer is indispensable to the glorifying of the Father.

So deep was the desire of Christ in the last night that his disciples should learn to believe in the power of his name and avail themselves of his promise of a sure and abundant answer, that we find the promise repeated seven times over. He knew how slow men are to believe in the wonderful promise of answer to prayer in his name. He longs to rouse a large and confident faith, to free our prayer from every shadow of a doubt, and to teach us to look upon intercession as the most certain and most blessed way of bringing glory to God, joy to our own souls, and blessing to the perishing world around us.

If we consider that such prayer is difficult to attain, we only need to remember what Christ told them. It was when the Holy Spirit came that they would have power to pray. It is to encourage us to yield to the control of the Spirit that he promised, "Ask and you shall receive, that your joy may be full." As we believe in the power of the Spirit working in us in full measure, intercession will become to us the joy and the strength of all our service.

When Paul wrote, "And whatever you do, in word or deed, do everything in the name of the Lord Jesus" (Col

3:17), he reminds us how everything in daily life is to bear the signature of the name of Jesus. As we learn to do this, we will say to the Father that as we live in that name before men we come to him confident that our prayer in that name will be answered. The life in fellowship with men is to be one with the life in fellowship with God. It is when the name of Jesus rules all in our life that it will empower our prayer.

21 Your Heavenly Father
Our Father who art in heaven. (Mt 6:9)

How simple, how beautiful, this invocation which Christ puts upon our lips! And yet how inconceivably rich in its meaning, in the fullness of the love and blessing it contains.

Just think what a book could be written of all the memories that there have been on earth of wise and loving fathers. Just think of what this world owes to the fathers who have made their children strong and happy in giving their lives to seek the welfare of their fellow men. And then think of how all this is but a shadow—a shadow of exquisite beauty, but still but a shadow of what the Father in heaven is to his children on earth.

What a gift Christ bestowed on us when he gave us the right to say: "Father!" "the Father of Christ," "our Father," "my Father."

And then, "our Father in heaven," our heavenly Father. We count it a great privilege as we bow in worship to know that the Father comes near to us where we are upon earth. But we soon begin to feel the need of rising up to enter into his holy presence in heaven, to breathe its atmosphere, to drink in its spirit, and to become truly heavenly-minded. And as we in the power of thought and imagination leave earth behind, and in the power of the Holy Spirit enter the holiest of all, where the seraphs worship, the word "heavenly Father" gains a new meaning, and our hearts come under an influence that can abide all the day.

And as we then gather up our thoughts of what fatherhood on earth has meant and hear the voice of Christ saying, "How much more," we sense the distance between the earthly picture and the heavenly reality, and can only bow in lowly, loving adoration, "Father, our Father, my Father." Only in this way can full joy and power come to us as we rest rejoicingly in the word, "How much more shall your heavenly Father give the Holy Spirit to those who ask him?"

May we have the grace to cultivate a heavenly spirit and daily to prove that we are children who have a Father in heaven, and who love day by day to dwell in his holy presence!

22 The Power of Prayer
The prayer of a righteous man has great power in its effects. (Jas 5:16)

Prayer has great power. It has great power with God. It has great power in the history of his Church and people. Prayer is the one great power which the Church can exercise in securing the working of God's omnipotence in the world.

The prayer of a righteous man has great power in its effects. That is, the prayer of a man who has the righteousness of Christ, not only as a garment covering him, but as a life-power inspiring him, as a new man "created after the likeness of God in true righteousness and holiness" (Eph 4:24); a man who lives as one of "the slaves of righteousness" (Rom 6:16, 18). These are the righteous whom the Lord loves and whose prayer has power (Ps 66:18, 19; 1 Jn 3:22). When Christ gave his great prayer promises in the last night, it was to those who keep his commandments. "If you love me, you will keep my commandments. And I will pray the Father, and he will give you another Counselor" (Jn 14:15, 16). "If you keep my commandments, you will abide in my love" (15:10). "If you abide in me, and my words abide in you, ask whatever you will, and it shall be done for you" (15:7).

"The prayer of a righteous man has great power in its effect." It is only when the righteous man stirs himself up and rouses his whole being to take hold of God that his prayer has great power. As Jacob said: "I will not let thee go"; as the importunate widow gave the just judge no rest, so it is that the effectual fervent prayer effects great things.

And then comes the effectual fervent prayer of many righteous. When two or three agree, there is the promise of an answer. How much more when hundreds and thousands unite with one accord to cry to God to display his mighty power on behalf of his people.

Let us join those who have united themselves to call upon God for the mighty power of his Holy Spirit in his Church. What a great and blessed work, and what a sure prospect, in God's time, of an abundant answer! Let us pray God individually and unitedly for the grace of the effectual fervent prayer which has great power in its effects.

23 Prayer and Sacrifice
I want you to know how greatly I strive for you.
(Col 2:1)

As men who are undertaking a great thing have to prepare themselves and summon all their powers to their aid, so Christians need to prepare themselves to pray "with their whole heart and strength." This is the law of the kingdom. Prayer needs sacrifice of ease, of time, of self. The secret of powerful prayer is sacrifice. It was thus with Christ Jesus, the great Intercessor. It is written of him, "When he makes himself an offering for sin, he shall see his offspring." "He shall see the fruit of the travail of his soul." "He shall divide the spoil with the strong, because he poured out his soul to death." In Gethsemane, "He offered up prayers and supplications with strong crying and tears." Prayer is sacrifice. David said: "Let my prayer be set forth before me as incense; and the lifting up of my hands as the evening sacrifice."

Prayer is sacrifice. Only because it is rooted in the sacrifice of Jesus Christ does prayer have worth. As he gave up everything in his prayer, "Thy will be done," our posture and disposition must ever be the offering up of everything to God and his service.

A pious Welsh miner had a relative whom the doctor ordered to Madeira. But there was no money. The miner resolved to take the little money that he had, and ventured to use it all. He procured a comfortable lodging at 7s. 6d per day for the invalid. He was content with tiny room for himself and lived on ten pence a day. He prayed until he was assured that the invalid would recover. On the last day of the month the sick one was well. When the miner reached home he said that he had now learned more than ever that the secret law and the hidden power of prayer lay in self-sacrifice.

Need we wonder at the lack of power in our prayer where there is so much reluctance to make the needful sacrifice in waiting upon God. Christ, the Christ we trust in, the Christ who lives in us, offered himself as a sacrifice to God. As this same spirit lives and rules in us, we shall receive power from him as intercessors to pray the prayer that has great power in its effects.

24 The Intercession of the Spirit for the Saints
He who searches the hearts of men knows what is the mind of the Spirit, because the Spirit intercedes for the saints according to the will of God. (Rom 8:27)

What a light these words cast upon the life of prayer in the hearts of the saints! We do not know how to pray as we ought. How often this hinders our prayer or hinders the faith that is essential to its success. But here we are encouraged that the Holy Spirit intercedes for us with groanings that cannot be uttered: "He intercedes for the saints according to the will of God."

What a prospect is here opened up to us! Where and how does the Spirit intercede for the saints? In no other way than that, in the heart that knows not what to pray, he secretly and effectually prays what is according to the will of God. This of course implies that we trust him to do his work in us, and that we wait before God even when we know what to pray, in the assurance that the Holy Spirit is praying in us. This further implies that we take time to tarry in God's presence, that we exercise an unbounded dependence upon the Holy Spirit who has been given to us to cry "Abba Father" within us, even when we have nothing to offer but groanings and sighs that cannot be uttered.

What a difference it would make in the life of many of

God's saints if they realized this! They have not only Jesus the Son of God, the great High Priest, ever living to intercede for them, and not only the liberty of asking in faith what they desire, and the promise that it shall be given them, but they actually have the Holy Spirit, "the Spirit of grace and supplication," to carry on, in the depths of their being, his work of interceding for them according to the will of God.

What a call to separate ourselves from the world, to yield ourselves wholeheartedly to the leading and praying of the Spirit within us, deeper than all our thoughts or expectations! What a call to surrender ourselves in stillness of soul, resting in the Lord and waiting patiently for him, as the Holy Spirit prays within us not only for ourselves, but especially for all saints according to the will of God.

25 That They All May Be One

Holy Father, keep them in thy name, which thou hast given me, that they may be one, even as we are one. . . . I do not pray for these only, but also for those who believe in me through their word, that they may all be one; even as thou, Father, art in me, and I in thee, that they also may be in us, . . . The glory which thou hast given me I have given to them, that they may be one even as we are one, I in them and thou in me, that they may become perfectly one, so that the world may know that thou hast sent me and hast loved them even as thou hast loved me. (Jn 17:11, 20-23)

Notice carefully how often the Lord used the expression, "that they may be one." He strongly emphasized these words, so we would realize the chief thought of his high priestly prayer. He longs for the words and the thought to have the same place in our hearts that they have in his. He wants us to understand that as he was on the way to go to the Father through the cross, he took the thought and the desire with him to heaven, to make it the object of his unceasing intercession there. And he entrusted these words to us, that we should take them into the world with us and make them the object of our unceasing intercession too. This alone enables us to fulfill his last, the new command, that we should love the brethren as he loved us, that our joy might be full.

How little the church has understood this. How little its different branches are marked by a fervent affectionate love for all the saints of whatever name or denomination. Shall we not heartily welcome the invitation to make this prayer, "that they may be one" a chief part of our daily fellowship with God? How simple it would be if we connected the two words, "Our Father," with all the children of God throughout the world. Each time we used these holy words we would only have to expand this little word "Our" into all the largeness and riches of God's fatherly love, and our hearts would soon learn as naturally as we say "Father" with the thought of his infinite love and our love for him, to say "Our" with childlike affection for all the saints of God, whoever and wherever they may be. The prayer that "they may be one" would then become a joy and a strength, a deeper bond of fellowship with Christ Jesus and all his saints, and an offer of a sweet savor to the Father of love.

26 The Disciples' Prayer
All these with one accord devoted themselves to prayer. (Acts 1:14)
They devoted themselves to the apostles' teaching and fellowship, to the breaking of bread and the prayers. (Acts 2:42)

What a lesson it would be to us in the school of prayer to have a clear apprehension of what this continuing with one accord in prayer meant to the disciples.

Consider the object of their desire. However defective their thoughts of the Spirit, this they knew, from the words of Jesus, "It is expedient for you that I go away"—that the Spirit would give the glorified Christ into their hearts in a way they had never known before. And it would be Christ himself, in the mighty power of God's Spirit, who would be their strength for the work to which he had called them.

With what confidence they expected the fulfillment of the promise. Had not the Master, who had loved them so well, assured them of what he would send upon them from the throne of the Father in heaven?

How persistently they pleaded in the midst of the praise and thanksgiving that filled their hearts as they worshipped their Lord in heaven, remembering all he had taught them about importunity, fully assured that however long the answer might be delayed he would fulfill their desires. Let us nourish our hearts with thoughts such as these, until we realize that the very same promise that was given to the disciples is given to us, and that we too, even though we have to cry day and night to God, can count upon the Father to answer our prayers.

And let us believe that as they continued with one accord in prayer, we also may unite as one man in presenting our petitions even though we cannot be together in one place. We can—in the love in which his Spirit makes us one, and in the experience of our Lord's presence with each one who joins with his brethren in praying in the name of Jesus—we can claim the promise that we too shall be filled with the Holy Spirit.

27 Paul's Call to Prayer
Keep alert with all perseverance, making supplication for all the saints and also for me. (Eph 6:18, 19)

Paul sensed the deep divine unity of the whole body of Christ and of the actual need of unceasing prayer for all the members of the body by all who belong to it. That he did not mean this to be an occasional thing, but the unceasing exercise of the life union in which they were bound together, is evident from the words he uses: "Pray . . . with all prayer and supplication," "Keep alert with all perseverance, making supplication for all the saints." He expects believers to be so conscious of being in Christ, and through him united consciously to the whole body, that in their daily life and all its engagements their highest aim would be the welfare of the body of Christ of which they had become members. He counted upon their being filled with the Spirit, so that it would be perfectly natural to them, without the thought of burden or constraint, to pray for all who belong to the body of Jesus Christ. As naturally as each member of my body is ready every moment to do what is needful for the welfare of the whole, even so, where the Holy Spirit has entire possession, the consciousness of union with Christ will be accompanied by the consciousness of the union, the joy, and the love of all the members.

Is not this what we need in our daily life, that every believer who has yielded himself undividedly to Christ Jesus day by day, every day, and all the day, live in the consciousness that he is one with Christ and his body? May the saints of God live for Christ their King, and also for all the members of that body of which he is the Head. May God's people be willing for this sacrifice of prayer and intercession at all times and for all saints!

28 Paul's Request for Prayer
And also for me, that utterance may be given me in opening my mouth boldly to proclaim the mystery of the gospel. (Eph 6:19, 20)

What light these words cast on the deep reality of Paul's faith in the absolute necessity and the wonderful power of prayer. He asks that they should pray "that utterance may be given me in opening my mouth boldly to proclaim the mystery of the gospel." Paul had now been a minister of the gospel for more than twenty years. One would think that he had such experience of preaching that it would come naturally to him to speak boldly. But so deep was his conviction of his own insufficiency and weakness, so absolute is his dependence on divine teaching and power, that he knew that without the direct help of God he could not do the work as it ought to be done. His sense of total and unalterable dependence upon God, who was with him, teaching him what and how to speak, was the ground of all his confidence and the keynote of his whole life.

But there is more. He had in all these twenty years, times without number, been in circumstances where he had to throw himself upon God alone, with no one to help him in prayer. Yet he had such deep spiritual insight into the unity of the body of Christ, and of his own actual dependence on the prayers of others, that he pleaded that they pray for him with all prayer and supplication in the Spirit. As little as a wrestler can afford to dispense with the help of the weakest members of his body in the struggle in which he is engaged, so little could Paul do without the prayers of the believers.

What a call to us in this twentieth century, to awaken to the consciousness that Christ our Intercessor in heaven, and all saints here upon earth, are engaged in one mighty contest, and that it is our duty to call out and to cultivate the gift of unceasing supplication for the power of God's Spirit in all his servants, that all may have divine utterance given them, and that all may speak boldly.

29 Prayer for All Saints

To the saints and faithful brethren in Christ at Colossae: . . . We always thank God, the Father of our Lord Jesus Christ, when we pray for you, because we have heard of your faith in Christ Jesus and of the love which you have for all the saints. . . . continue steadfastly in prayer, being watchful in it with thanksgiving; and pray for us also. (Col 1:1-4; 4:2, 3)

Prayer for all saints: let this be our first thought. It will take time, thought, and love to realize what is included in that simple expression. Think of your own neighborhood and the saints you know; think of your whole country, and praise God for all who are his saints; think of all the nations and the saints of God to be found among them in ever-increasing numbers.

Think of all the different circumstances and conditions in which these are to be found, and all the varying needs which call for God's grace and help. Think of those who are God's saints, and yet through ignorance or laziness, through worldly-mindedness or unbelief, are walking in the dark and bringing no honor to God. Think of those who are in earnest, and yet conscious of a life of failure, with little or no power to please God or to bless man. And then think of those who are to be found everywhere, in solitary places or in companies, whose one aim is to serve the Lord who bought them and to be the light of those around them. Think of them especially as joining, often unconscious of their relation to the whole body of Christ, in pleading for the great promise of the Holy Spirit and the love and oneness of heart which he alone can give.

This is not the work of one day or one night. It needs a heart which will set itself from time to time to seriously consider the state and the need of that body of Christ to which we belong. But when once we begin, we will see what abundant reason there is for our persevering and yielding to God's Spirit, that he may equip us for the great and blessed work of day by day praying the twofold prayer, for the love of God and Christ to fill the hearts of his people, and for the power of the Holy Spirit to descend down and accomplish God's work in this sinful world.

30 Prayer by All Saints
He will deliver us. . . . You also must help us by prayer. (2 Cor 1:10, 11)
Some indeed preach Christ from envy and rivalry. . . . I know that through your prayers and the help of the Spirit of Jesus Christ this will turn out for my deliverance.
(Phil 1:15, 19)

This subject calls us once again to think of all saints throughout the world, but leads us to view them from a different standpoint. If we are to ask God to increase the number and the power of those who do pray, we will form some impression of the hope that our circle of intercessors may gradually increase in number and power.

Our first thoughts will naturally turn to the multitude of the saints who think and know very little about the duty or the blessedness of pleading for the body of Christ, or for all the work which has to be done to perfect its members. We shall then remember how many do intercede for the power of his Spirit, but whose thoughts are chiefly limited to spheres of work that they are acquainted with or directly interested in.

This leaves us with what is, comparatively speaking, a very limited number of those who will be ready to take part very limited number of those who will be ready to take part in the prayer which ought to be sent up by the whole Church, for the unity of the body and the power of the Spirit. And even then it may be only a small number who are really drawn and urged to take part in this daily prayer for the outpouring of the Spirit on all God's people.

And yet many may feel that the proposal meets a long-felt need, and that it is an unspeakable privilege, whether with few or many, to make Christ's last prayer, "that they may be one," the daily supplication of our faith and love. It may be that in time believers will band together in small circles, or throughout wider districts, to rouse those around them to take part in the great work that the prayer for all saints may become one by all saints.

This message is for all who desire it, and who seek to prove their consecration to their Lord in the unceasing daily supplication for the power of his love and Spirit to be revealed to all his people.

31 Prayer for All the Fullness of the Spirit

Bring the full tithes into the storehouse, that there may be food in my house; and thereby put me to the test, says the Lord of hosts, if I will not open the windows of heaven for you and pour down for you an overflowing blessing. (Mal 3:10)

This last promise in the Old Testament tells us how abundant the blessing is to be. Pentecost was only the beginning of what God was willing to do. The promise of the Father, as Christ gave it, still waits for its perfect fulfillment. Let us attempt to realize how free we are to ask for and to expect great things.

Just as the great command to go and preach the gospel was not only meant for the disciples but for us too, so the very last command, "Wait until you receive power from on high," "Wait for the promise of the Father," "You shall be baptized with the Holy Spirit," is also for us, and is the ground for the confident assurance that our prayer with one accord will be heard.

Consider all the needs throughout the whole Church and

its missions, and realize that the only remedy for inefficiency or impotence, which will enable us to gain the victory over the powers of this world of darkness, is the manifest presence of our Lord in the midst of his hosts and in the power of his Spirit. Let us take time to consider the state of the Church until we are brought to the conviction that nothing will help except the supernatural, almighty intervention of our Lord himself, to rouse his hosts for the great battle against evil. Can anyone conceive or suggest any other matter for prayer that can at all compete with this: for the power of God on the ministers of the gospel, and on all his people, to endue them with power from on high to make the gospel the power of God for salvation?

As we unite the prayer for the whole Church on earth with the prayer for the whole power of God in heaven, we will know that the greatest truths of the heavenly world and the kingdom of God possess us, and that we are indeed asking for what God is longing to give, as soon as he finds hearts utterly yielded to himself in faith and obedience.

Month Six

1 Every Day
Give us each day our daily bread. (Lk 11:3)

Some Christians consider the idea of praying every day as altogether beyond them.

They could not undertake it, and yet they pray to God to give them their bread day by day. Surely if a child of God has once yielded himself with his whole life to God's love and service, he should count it a privilege to take advantage of any invitation that would help him every day to come into God's presence with the great need of his Church and kingdom.

Many desire to live wholly for God. They acknowledge that Christ gave himself for them, and that his love now watches over them and works in them without ceasing. They admit that nothing less than the measure of the love of Christ for us is to be the measure of our love for him. They know that if this is to be the standard of their lives, they ought to welcome every opportunity to devote their heart's strength to the interests of Christ's kingdom and to the prayer that can bring down God's blessing.

Our invitation to daily united prayer may come to some as a new and perhaps unexpected opportunity of becoming God's remembrancers. Think of the privilege of being allowed to plead every day with God on behalf of his saints for the outpouring of his Spirit, of praying for the coming of his kingdom, that his will may be done on earth as it is in heaven. To those who have little understood the privilege and the solemn duty of waiting on God in prayer for his blessing on the world, the invitation ought to be most welcome. And even to those who have already their special circles of work for which to pray, the thought of enlarging their vision and their hearts to include all God's saints and all the work of his kingdom, and the promise of an abundant outpouring of his Spirit, should urge them to take part in a ministry by which their other work will not suffer, but their hearts be strengthened with a joy and a love and a faith that they have never known before.

2 With One Accord
They were all together in one place. . . . And they were all filled with the Holy Spirit. (Acts 2:1, 4)

The previous chapters concerned the solidarity of the whole body of Christ and the need of the deliberate cultivation of the slumbering or buried talents of intercession. We may indeed thank God, for we know of the tens of thousands of his children who in daily prayer are pleading for some portion of the work of God's kingdom in which they are personally interested. But in many cases there is a lack of that large-hearted and universal love that embraces all the saints of God and their service. There is not the boldness and the strength that comes from the consciousness of being part of a large and conquering army under the leadership of our conquering King.

We said that a wrestler in the games gathers up his whole strength and counts upon every member of his body doing its very utmost. In a war, each detachment of soldiers not only throws its whole heart into the work that it has to do, but it rejoices in and is encouraged by the bravery of the far-distant members of the one great army. Do we not need, in the Church of Christ, such an enthusiasm for the King and his kingdom and such a faith in his purpose to make his name known to every human being, that our prayers would rise up every day, with a large-hearted love that grasps the whole body of Christ and pleads daily for the power of the

Holy Spirit on all its members, even to the very feeblest?

The strength unity gives is inconceivable. The power of each individual member is increased to a large degree by the inspiration of fellowship with a large and conquering host. Nothing can so help us to an ever-larger faith as the consciousness of being one body and one spirit in Christ Jesus. It was as the disciples were all with one accord in one place on the day of Pentecost, that they were all filled with the Holy Spirit. United prayer brings the answer to prayer.

3 A Personal Call
He delivered us . . . on him we have set our hope that he will deliver us again. (2 Cor 1:9, 10)
Some indeed preach Christ from envy and rivalry. . . . I know that through your prayers and the help of the Spirit of Jesus Christ this will turn out for my deliverance. (Phil 1:16, 19)

Texts like these prove that there were still Christians in the churches under the full power of the Holy Spirit, on whom Paul could count for effectual prayer. When we plead with Christians to pray without ceasing, there are a very large number who quietly decide that such a life is not possible for them. They think they have no special gift for prayer; they do not have that intense desire for glorifying Christ in the salvation of souls; they have not yet learned what it is, under the power of the constraining love of Christ, to live not for themselves, but for him who died for them and rose again.

And yet it is such that we call to offer themselves in a wholehearted surrender to live entirely for Christ. We ask them whether they are ashamed of the selfish life that simply uses Christ as a convenience to escape from hell and secure a place in heaven. We assure them that God can change their lives and fill their hearts with Christ and his Holy Spirit. We plead with them to believe that with God all things are possible. He is able and willing, indeed most anxious, to restore them to the joy of the Father's presence and service.

One step on the way for men and women to attain this

will be for them to respond to the call to every day and all the day, in the power of Christ's abiding presence, live in the spirit of unceasing intercession for all saints, that they receive the power of the Holy Spirit, and acknowledge that this is nothing less than a duty, a sacrifice that Christ's love has a right to claim, and that he by his Spirit will indeed work in them. The man, however far he may have come short, who accepts the call as coming from Christ and draws near to God in humble prayer for the needed grace, will have taken the first step in the path that leads to fellowship with God, to a new faith and life in Christ Jesus, and to the surrender of his whole being to the intercession of the Spirit which will bring Pentecost again into the hearts of God's people.

4 The Redemption of the Cross
Christ redeemed us from the curse of the law, having become a curse for us. (Gal 3:13)

Scripture teaches us that there are two points of view from which we may regard Christ's death upon the cross.

The first is the redemption of the cross: Christ dying for us as our complete deliverance from the curse of sin. The other is the fellowship of the cross: Christ taking us up to die with him and making us partakers of the fellowship of his death in our own experience.

In our text we have three great unsearchable thoughts. The law of God has pronounced a curse on all sin and on all that is sinful. Christ took our curse upon him, yes, became a curse, and destroyed its power. And in that cross we now have the everlasting redemption from sin and all its power. The cross reveals to us man's sin, as under the curse, Christ becoming a curse and so overcoming it, and our full and everlasting deliverance from the curse.

In these thoughts the most hopeless sinner finds sure grounds for confidence and hope. God had indeed in Paradise pronounced a curse upon this earth and all that belongs to it. On Mount Ebal, in connection with the giving of the law, half of the people of Israel were twelve times over to pronounce a curse on all sin (Dt 27:15-20).

And there was to be in their midst a continual reminder of it. "If a man has committed a crime punishable by death . . . and you hang him on a tree, his body shall not remain all night upon the tree, but you shall bury him the same day, for a hanged man is accursed by God" (Dt 21:22-23). And yet who could ever have thought that the Son of God himself would die upon the accursed tree and become a curse for us? But such is the gospel of God's love, and the penitent sinner can now rejoice in the confident assurance that the curse is forever put away from all who believe in Christ Jesus.

The preaching of the redemption of the cross is the foundation and center of the salvation the gospel brings us. To those who believe its full truth it is a cause of unceasing thanksgiving. It gives us boldness to rejoice in God. There is nothing which will keep the heart more tender towards God, enabling us to live in his love and to make him known to those who have not yet found him. May God be praised for the redemption of the cross!

5 The Fellowship of the Cross
Have this mind among yourselves, which is yours in Christ Jesus. (Phil 2:5)

Paul here tells us what that mind was in Christ: he emptied himself; he took the form of a servant ; he humbled himself, even to the death of the cross. It is this mind that was in Christ, the deep humility that gave up his life to the very death, that is to be the spirit that animates us. In this way we will prove and enjoy the blessed fellowship of his cross.

Paul had said in verse 1: "So if there is any encouragement in Christ"—the Comforter was to reveal his real presence in them—"any participation in the Spirit"—it was in this power of the Spirit that they were to breathe the Spirit of the crucified Christ and manifest his disposition in the fellowship of the cross in their lives.

As they strove to do this, they would experience their need of a deeper insight into their real oneness with Christ. They would learn to appreciate the truth that they had been crucified with Christ, that their "old man" had been crucified, and that they had died to sin in Christ's death and were now living to God in his life. They would learn to know what it meant that the crucified Christ lived in them, and that they had crucified the flesh with its affections and lusts. It was because the crucified Jesus lived in them that they could live crucified to the world.

And so they would gradually enter more deeply into the meaning and the power of their high calling—to live as those who were dead to sin and the world and self. Each in his own measure would bear about in his life the marks of the cross, with its sentence of death on the flesh, with its hating of the self-life and its entire denial of self, with its growing conformity to the crucified Redeemer in his deep humility and entire surrender of his will to the life of God.

It is no easy school and no hurried learning, this school of the cross. But it will lead to a deeper comprehension of and a higher appreciation for the redemption of the cross through the personal experience of the fellowship of the cross.

6 Crucified with Christ
I have been crucified with Christ; it is no longer I who live, but Christ who lives in me. (Gal 2:20)

The thought of fellowship with Christ in his cross has often led to the vain attempt in our own power to follow him and bear his image. But this is impossible to man until he first learns to know something of what it means to say, "I have been crucified with Christ."

When Adam died, all his descendants died with him and in him. In his sin in Paradise, and in the spiritual death into which he fell, I had a share; I died in him. And the power of that sin and death, in which all his descendants share, works in every child of Adam every day.

Christ came as the second Adam. In his death on the cross, all who believe in him had a share. Each one may truly say, "I have been crucified with Christ." As the representative of his people, he took them up with him on the cross, and me, too. The life that he gives is the crucified life in which he entered heaven and was exalted to the throne, standing as a Lamb that had been slain. The power of his death and life work in me, and as I hold fast the truth that I have been crucified with him, and now I myself live no more but Christ lives in me, I receive power to conquer sin; the life that I have received from him is a life that has been crucified and freed from the power of sin.

This is a deep and very great truth, but most Christians have little knowledge of it. And this knowledge is not gained easily or speedily. It requires a great longing to die to all sin. It takes a strong faith, wrought by the Holy Spirit, that the union with Christ crucified and the fellowship of his cross can day by day become our life. The life that he lives in heaven has its strength and its glory in the fact that it is a crucified life. And the life that he imparts to the believing disciple is also a crucified life with its victory over sin and its power of access into God's presence.

It is true that I no longer live, but Christ lives in me as the Crucified One. As faith realizes and holds fast the fact that the crucified Christ lives in me, life in the fellowship of the cross becomes a possibility and a blessed experience.

7 Crucified to the World
But far be it from me to glory except in the cross of our Lord Jesus Christ, by which the world has been crucified to me, and I to the world. (Gal 6:14)

What Paul had written in Galatians 2 is confirmed here in the end of the epistle and expressed still more strongly.

He speaks of his only glory being that in Christ he has been crucified to the world and entirely delivered from its power. When he said, "I have been crucified with Christ," it was not only an inner spiritual truth, but an actual, practical experience in relation to the world and its temptations. Christ had spoken about the world hating him, and his having overcome the world; Paul knew that the world which nailed Christ to the cross had also done the same to him. He boasts that he lives as one crucified to the world and that the world as an impotent enemy was crucified to him. It was this that made him glory in the cross of Christ. It had wrought out a complete deliverance from the world.

How very different the relation of Christians to the world in our day! They agree that they may not commit the sins that the world allows. But they are good friends with the world and feel free to enjoy as much of it as they can, if they only keep from open sin. They do not realize that the most dangerous source of sin is the love of the world with its lusts and pleasures.

When the world crucified Christ, it crucified you with him. When Christ overcame the world on the cross, he made you an overcomer too. He calls you now, at whatever cost of self-denial, to regard the world, in its hostility to God and his kingdom, as a crucified enemy over whom the cross can ever keep you conqueror.

What a different relationship to the pleasures and attractions of the world the Christian has who by the Holy Spirit has learned to say, "I have been crucified with Christ; it is no longer I who live but Christ who lives in me!" Let us fervently pray that the Holy Spirit, through whom Christ offered himself on the cross, may reveal to us in power what it means to "glory in the cross of our Lord Jesus Christ, by which the world has been crucified to me, and I to the world."

8 The Flesh Crucified
Those who belong to Christ Jesus have crucified the flesh with its passions and desires. (Gal 5:24)

Of the flesh Paul teaches us, "I know that nothing good dwells within me, that is, in my flesh" (Rom 7:18). And again, "The mind that is set on the flesh is hostile to God; it does not submit to God's law, indeed it cannot" (Rom 8:7). When Adam lost the Spirit of God, he became flesh. The "flesh" is the evil, corrupt nature that we inherit from Adam. Of this flesh it is written, "Our old self was crucified with him" (Rom 6:6). And Paul puts it here even more strongly: "They that are in Christ Jesus have crucified the flesh."

When the disciples heard and obeyed the call of Jesus to follow him, they honestly meant to do so; but as he later taught them what that would mean, they were far from ready to yield immediate obedience. And even so those who are Christ's and have accepted him as the Crucified One, little understand what that includes. By that act of surrender they actually have crucified the flesh and consented to regard it as an accursed thing, nailed to the cross of Christ.

How many there are who have never for a moment thought of such a thing! It may be that the preaching of Christ crucified has been defective. Or perhaps the truth of our being crucified with Christ has not been taught. Many shrink back from the self-denial that it implies, and as a result, where the flesh is allowed in any measure to have its way, the Spirit of Christ cannot exert his power.

Paul taught the Galatians: "Walk by the Spirit, and do not gratify the desires of the flesh." "As many as are led by the Spirit of God, they are the children of God." And the Spirit can alone guide us as the flesh, in living faith and fellowship with Christ Jesus, is kept in the place of crucifixion.

Lord, how little I understood when I accepted you in faith that I crucified once for all the flesh with its passions and lusts! Teach me to so believe and live in you, the Crucified One, that with Paul I may ever glory in the cross on which the world and the flesh are crucified.

9 Bearing the Cross
He who does not take his cross and follow me is not worthy of me. He who finds his life will lose it, and he who loses his life for my sake will find it. (Mt 10:38-39)

We have had some of Paul's great words to the Galatians about the cross and our being crucified with Christ. Let us now turn to the Master himself to hear what he has to teach us. We shall find that what Paul could teach openly and fully after the crucifixion, the Master gave in words that could at first hardly be understood, and yet contained the seed of the full truth.

It was in the ordination charge, when Christ sent forth his disciples, that he first said that each disciple must take up his cross and follow him.

The only meaning the disciples could attach to these

words was from what they had often seen, when an evil-doer who had been sentenced to death by the cross was led out bearing his cross to the place of execution. In bearing the cross, he acknowledged the sentence of death that was on him. And Christ would have his disciples understand that their nature was so evil and corrupt that it was only in losing their natural life that they could find the true life. Of himself it was true; all his life he bore his cross, the sentence of death that he knew to rest upon himself on account of our sins. And so he would have his disciple bear his cross, the sentence of death upon himself and his evil, carnal nature.

The disciples could not at once understand all this. But Christ gave them seed words, which would germinate in their hearts and later on begin to reveal their full meaning. The disciple was not only to carry the sentence of death in himself but to learn that in following the Master to his cross, he would find the power to lose his life and to receive instead of it the life that would come through the cross of Christ.

Christ asks his disciples to forsake all and take up their cross, give up their whole will and life, and follow him. The call comes to us, too, to give up the self-life with its self-pleasing and self-exaltation, and bear the cross in fellowship with him. Then we will partake of his victory.

10 Self-Denial
Then Jesus told his disciples, "If any man would come after me, let him deny himself and take up his cross and follow me." (Mt 16:24)

Christ had for the first time definitely announced that he would have to suffer much and be killed and be raised again. Peter rebuked him, saying, "God forbid, Lord! This shall never happen to you." Christ's answer was, "Get behind me, Satan." The spirit of Peter, seeking to turn him away from the cross and its suffering, was nothing but Satan tempting Jesus to turn aside from the path which God had appointed as our way of salvation.

Christ then adds the words of our text, in which he uses

for the second time the words "take up the cross." But with that he uses a most significant expression revealing what is implied in the cross: "If any man would come after me, let him deny himself and take up his cross and follow me." When Adam sinned, he fell out of the life of heaven and of God into the life of the world and of self. Self-pleasing, self-sufficiency, self-exaltation became the law of his life. Jesus Christ, "though he was in the form of God, emptied himself, taking the form of a servant, . . . and humbled himself . . . and became obedient unto death, even death on a cross." What he has done himself he asks of all who desire to follow him: "If any man would come after me, let him deny himself."

Instead of denying himself, Peter denied his Lord: "I know not the man." When a man learns to obey Christ's commands, he says of himself: "I know not the man." It is the secret of true discipleship, to bear the cross, to acknowledge the death sentence that has been passed on self, and to deny any right that self has to rule over us.

Death to self is to be the Christian's watchword. The surrender to Christ is to be so entire, the surrender for Christ's sake to live for those around us so complete, that self is never allowed to come down from the cross to which it has been crucified, but is ever kept in the place of death.

Listen to the voice of Jesus: "Deny self." Ask that by the grace of the Holy Spirit, as the disciples of Christ who denied himself for us, we may ever live as those in whom self has been crucified with Christ, and in whom the crucified Christ now lives as Lord and Master.

11 He Cannot Be My Disciple

If any one comes to me and does not hate . . . his own life, he cannot be my disciple. Whoever does not bear his own cross and come after me, cannot be my disciple. . . . Whoever of you does not renounce all that he has cannot be my disciple. (Lk 14:26-27, 33)

For the third time Christ speaks about bearing the cross. He gives new meaning to it when he says that a man must hate his own life and renounce all he has. Three times he solemnly repeats the words that without this a man cannot be his disciple.

"If a man hate not his own life." And why does Christ make such an exacting demand the condition of discipleship? Because the sinful nature we have inherited from Adam is indeed so vile and full of sin, that if our eyes were only opened to see it in its true nature, we would flee from it as loathsome and incurably evil. "The flesh is enmity against God"; the soul that seeks to love God cannot but hate the old man which is corrupt through its whole being. Nothing less than this, the hating of our own life, will make us willing to bear the cross, and carry within us the sentence of death on our evil nature. It is not until we hate this life with a deadly hatred that we will be ready to give up the old nature to die the death that is its due.

Christ has one word more: "Whoever of you does not renounce all that he has," whether in property or character, "cannot be my disciple." Christ claims all. Christ undertakes to satisfy every need and to give a hundred-fold more than we give up. It is when by faith we become conscious of what it means to know Christ, and to love him and to receive from him what enriches and satisfies our immortal spirits, that we shall count the surrender of what at first appeared so difficult, our highest privilege. As we learn what it means that Christ is our life, we shall count all things as loss because of the surpassing worth of knowing Christ Jesus our Lord. In the path of following him, and ever learning to know and to love him better, we shall willingly sacrifice all, self with its life, to make room for him who is more than all.

12 Follow Me

And Jesus looking upon him loved him, and said to him, "You lack one thing; go, sell what you have, and give to the poor, and you will have treasure in heaven; and come, follow me." (Mk 10:21)

When Christ spoke these words to the young ruler, he went away grieved. Jesus said: "How hard it will be for those who have riches to enter the kingdom of God!" The disciples were astonished at his words. When Christ repeated once again what he had said, they were astonished beyond measure. "Who then can be saved?" "Jesus, looking upon them said, 'With men it is impossible, but not with God; for all things are possible with God.'"

Christ had spoken about bearing the cross from the human side, as the one condition of discipleship. Here with the rich young ruler he reveals from the side of God what is needed to give men the will and the power to sacrifice all, if they were to enter the kingdom. He said to Peter, when he had confessed him as Christ, the Son of God, that flesh and blood had not revealed it unto him, but his Father in heaven, to remind him and the other disciples that it was only by divine teaching that he could make the confession. So here with the ruler, he unveils the great mystery that it is only by divine power that a man can take up his cross, can lose his life, can deny himself and hate the life to which he is by nature so attached.

What multitudes have sought to follow Christ and obey his injunction, and have found that they have utterly failed! What multitudes have felt that Christ's claims were beyond their reach and have sought to be Christians without any attempt at the wholehearted devotion and the entire self-denial which Christ asks for!

Let us in our study of what the fellowship of the cross means take today's lesson to heart and believe that it is only by putting our trust in the living God and the mighty power in which he is willing to work in the heart, that we can attempt to be disciples who forsake all and follow Christ in the fellowship of his cross.

13 A Grain of Wheat

Truly, truly, I say to you, unless a grain of wheat falls into the earth and dies, it remains alone; but if it dies, it bears much fruit. He who loves his life loses it, and he who hates his life in this world will keep it for eternal life. (Jn 12:24, 25)

All nature is the parable of how the losing of a life can be the way to secure a truer and a higher life. Every grain of wheat, every seed throughout the world, teaches the lesson that through death lies the path to beautiful and fruitful life.

It was so with the Son of God. He had to pass through death, in all its bitterness and suffering, before he could rise to heaven and impart his life to his redeemed people. And here under the shadow of the approaching cross he calls his disciples: "If any one serves me, he must follow me." He repeats the words: "He who hates his life in this world will keep it for eternal life."

One might have thought that Christ did not need to lose his holy life before he could find it again. But so it was: God laid upon him the iniquity of us all, and he yielded to the inexorable law: Through death to life and to fruit.

How much more ought we, in the consciousness of that evil nature and that death which we inherited in Adam, be willing, even most grateful, that there is a way open to us by which, in the fellowship of Christ and his cross, we can die to this accursed self! With what gratitude ought we to listen to the call to bear our cross, to yield our "old man" as crucified with Christ daily to that death which he deserves! Surely the thought that the power of the eternal Life is working in us ought to make us willing and glad to die the death that brings us into the fellowship and the power of life in a risen Christ.

How little this is understood! Let us believe that what is impossible to man is possible to God. Let us believe that the law of the Spirit of Christ Jesus, the Risen Lord, can indeed make his death and his life the daily experience of our souls.

14 Thy Will Be Done
My Father, if it be possible, let this cup pass from me; nevertheless, not as I will, but as thou wilt. (Mt 26:39)

The death of Christ on the cross is the highest and the holiest that can be known of him even in the glory of heaven. And the highest and the holiest that the Holy Spirit can work in us is to take us up and to keep us in the fellowship of the cross of Christ. We need to enter deeply into the truth that Christ the beloved Son of the Father could not return to the glory of heaven until he had first given himself over to death. As this great truth opens up to us, it will help us to understand how in our life, and in our fellowship with Christ, it is impossible for us to share his life until we have first surrendered ourselves every day to die to sin and the world, and so to abide in the unbroken fellowship with our crucified Lord.

And it is from Christ alone that we can learn what it means to have fellowship with his sufferings and to be conformed unto his death. When in the agony of Gethsemane he considered what it would mean to die the accursed death under the power of sin, with God's countenance so turned from him that not a single ray of its light could penetrate the darkness, he prayed that the cup might pass from him. But when no answer came, and he understood that the Father could not allow the cup to pass by, he yielded up his whole will and life in the words, "Thy will be done." In these words of your Lord in his agony, you can enter into fellowship with him, and in his strength your own heart will be strengthened to believe most confidently that God in his omnipotence will enable you to yield everything, because you have indeed been crucified with Christ.

"Thy will be done"; let these be the deepest and the highest words in your life. In the power of Christ, with whom you have been crucified, and in the power of his Spirit, the definite daily surrender to the will of God will become the joy and the strength of your life.

15 The Love of the Cross
And Jesus said, "Father, forgive them; for they know not what they do." (Lk 23:34)

The seven words on the cross reveal the mind of Christ and show the dispositions that become his disciples. Take the three first words, all the expression of his wonderful love.

"Father, forgive them; for they know not what they do." He prays for his enemies. In the hour of their triumph over him, and of the shame and suffering which they delight in showering on him, he pours out his love in prayer for them. Everyone who believes in a crucified Christ is to go and do likewise, even as he has said, "Love your enemies, do good to those who hate you, bless those who curse you, and pray for those who persecute you." The law of the Master is the law for the disciples; the love of the crucified Jesus, the only rule for those who believe in him.

"Woman, behold thy son!" "Behold thy mother!" The love that cared for his enemies, cared too for his friends. Jesus felt what the anguish must be in the heart of his widowed mother, and commits her to the care of the beloved disciple. He knew that for John there could be no higher privilege, and no more blessed service, than that of taking his place in the care of Mary. Even so we who are the disciples of Christ must not only pray for his enemies, but prove our love to him, and to all who belong to him, by seeing to it that every solitary one is comforted, and that every loving heart has some work to do in caring for those who belong to the Master.

"Truly, I say to you, today you will be with me in Paradise." The penitent thief had appealed to Christ's mercy to remember him. With what readiness of joy and love Christ immediately answers his prayer! Whether it was the love that prayed for his enemies, or the love that cared for his friends, or the love that rejoices over the penitent sinner who was being cast out by man—in all Christ proves that the cross is a cross of love, that the Crucified One is the embodiment of a love that passes knowledge.

With every thought of what we owe to that love, with every act of faith in which we rejoice in its redemption, let us prove that the mind of the crucified Christ is our mind, and that his love is not only what we trust in for ourselves, but what guides us in our loving fellowship with the world around us.

16 The Sacrifice of the Cross

My God, my God, why hast thou forsaken me? (Mt 27:46)
I thirst. . . . It is finished. (Jn 19:28, 30)

The three first words on the cross reveal love in its outflow to men. The next three reveal love in the tremendous sacrifice that it brought, to deliver us from our sins and give the victory over every foe. They will still reveal the very mind that was in Christ, and that is to be in us as the disposition of our whole life.

"My God, my God, why hast thou forsaken me?" How deep must have been the darkness that overshadowed him, when not one ray of light could pierce, and he could not say, "My Father!" It was this awful desertion, breaking in upon that life of childlike fellowship with the Father in which he had always walked, that caused him the agony and the bloody sweat in Gethsemane. "O my Father, let this cup pass from me"—but it might not be, and he bowed his head in submission: "Thy will be done." It was his love for God and love for man, yielding himself to the very uttermost. It is as we learn to believe and to worship that love, that we too shall learn to say: "Abba, Father, Thy will be done."

"I thirst." The body now expresses the terrible experience of what it passed through when the fire of God's wrath against sin came upon Christ in the hour of his desertion. He had spoken of Dives crying: "I am tormented in this flame." Christ utters his complaint of what he had suffered. Physicians tell us that in crucifixion the whole body is in agony with a terrible fever and pain. Our Lord endured it all and cried: "I thirst"; soul and body was the sacrifice he brought the Father.

And then comes the great word: "It is finished." All that there was to suffer and endure had been brought a willing sacrifice; he had finished the work the Father gave him to do. His love held nothing back. He gave himself an offering and a sacrifice. Such was the mind of Christ, and such must be the disposition of everyone who owes himself and his life to that sacrifice. The mind that was in Christ must be in us ready to say: "I have come to do the will of him who sent me, and to finish his work." And every day as we grow more confident in Christ's finished work, we must see our heart more entirely yielding itself like him, a whole burnt offering in the service of God and his love.

17 The Death of the Cross
"Father, into thy hands I commit my spirit!" And having said this he breathed his last. (Lk 23:46)

Like David (Ps 31:5), Christ had often committed his spirit into the hands of his Father for his daily life and need. But here is something new and very special. He gives up his spirit into the power of death, gives up all control over it, to sink down into the darkness and death of the grave, where he can neither think, nor pray, nor will. He surrenders himself to the utmost into the Father's hands, trusting him to care for him in the dark and in due time to raise him up again.

If we have indeed died in Christ and are now in faith every day to carry about with us the death of our Lord Jesus, this word is the very one that we need. Just think once again what Christ meant when he said that we must hate and lose our life.

We died in Adam; the life we receive from him is death; there is nothing good or heavenly in our fallen nature. It is to this inward evil nature, to all the life that we have from this world, that we must die. There cannot be any thought of real holiness, without totally dying to this self or "old man." Many deceive themselves because they seek to be alive in God before they are dead to their own nature: a thing as impossible as it is for a grain of wheat to be alive before it dies. This total dying to self lies at the root of all true piety. The spiritual life must grow out of death.

And if we ask how we can do this, we find the answer in the mind in which Christ died. Like him we cast ourselves upon God, without knowing how the new life is to be attained; but as we, in fellowship with Jesus say, "Father, into thy hands I commit my spirit," and depend simply and absolutely upon God to raise us up into the new life, there will be fulfilled in us the wonderful promise of God's Word, concerning the exceeding greatness of his power in us who believe, according to the mighty power which he wrought in Christ when he raised him from the dead.

This indeed is the true rest of faith, that lives every day

and every hour in the absolute dependence upon the continual and immediate quickening of the divine life in us by God himself through the Holy Spirit.

18 It Is Finished
When Jesus had received the vinegar, he said, "It is finished." (Jn 19:30)

The seven words of our Lord on the cross reveal to us his mind and disposition. At the beginning of his ministry he said: "My food is to do the will of him who sent me, and to accomplish his work" (Jn 4:34). In all things, the small as well as the great, he should accomplish God's work. In the high-priestly prayer at the end of the three years' ministry, he could say: "I glorified thee on earth, having accomplished the work which thou gavest me to do" (Jn 17:4). He sacrificed all and in dying on the cross could truly say, "It is finished."

With that word to the Father he laid down his life. With that word he was strengthened, after the terrible agony on the cross, in the knowledge that all was now fulfilled. And with that word he uttered the truth of the gospel of our redemption, that all that was needed for man's salvation had been accomplished on the cross.

This disposition should characterize every follower of Christ. The mind that was in him must be in us—it must be our meat, the strength of our life, to do the will of God in all things, and to finish his work. There may be small things about which we are not conscientious and so we harm ourselves and God's work. Or we draw back before some great thing which demands too much sacrifice. In every case we may find strength to perform our duty in Christ's word, "It is finished." His finished work secured the victory over every foe. By faith we may appropriate that dying word of Christ on the cross and find the power for daily living and dying in the fellowship of the crucified Christ.

Study the inexhaustible treasure contained in this word, "It is finished." Faith in what Christ accomplished on the cross will enable you to manifest in daily life the spirit of the cross.

19 Dead to Sin
How can we who died to sin still live in it? (Rom 6:2)

After having, in the first section of the epistle to the Romans (1:16 to 5:11), expounded the great doctrine of justification by faith, Paul proceeds, in the second section (5:12 to 8:39), to unfold the related doctrine of the new life by faith in Christ. Taking Adam as a figure of Christ, he teaches that just as we all really and actually died in Adam, so that his death reigns in our nature, even so in Christ those who believe in him actually and effectually died to sin, were freed from it, and became partakers of the new holy life of Christ.

He asks, "How can we who died to sin still live in it?" In these words we have the deep spiritual truth that our death to sin in Christ delivers us from its power, so that we no longer may or need to live in it. The secret of true and full holiness is faith, and, by in the power of the Holy Spirit, to living in the consciousness that I am dead to sin.

In expounding this truth he reminds them that they were baptized into the death of Christ. We were buried with him through baptism into death. We were united with him by the likeness of his death. Our "old man" was crucified with him, that the body of sin might be rendered void and powerless. Take time and quietly, asking for the teaching of the Holy Spirit, to ponder these words until the truth masters you: I am indeed dead to sin in Christ Jesus. As we grow in the consciousness of our union with the crucified Christ, we shall experience the power of his life in us, freeing us from the power of sin.

Romans 6 is one of the most blessed portions of the New Testament of our Lord Jesus; it teaches us that our "old man," the old nature that is in us, was actually crucified with him, so that now we need no longer be in bondage to sin. But remember that it is only as the Holy Spirit makes Christ's death a reality within us, that we shall know, not by force of argument or conviction, but in the reality of the power of a divine life, that we are indeed dead to sin. It only needs the continual living in Christ Jesus.

20 The Righteousness of God
*Abraham believed God, and it was reckoned to him
as righteousness. . . . the God in whom he believed, who gives
life to the dead.* (Rom 4:3, 17)

Let us now, after listening to the words of our Lord Jesus
about our fellowship with him in the cross, turn to St. Paul,
and see how through the Holy Spirit he gives a deeper
insight into what our death in Christ means.

The first section of Romans is devoted to the doctrine of
justification by faith in Christ. After speaking of the sin of
the Gentiles (1:18-32), and then of the sin of the Jews
(2:1-29), he points out how both Jew and Gentile are
"guilty before God." "All have sinned and come short." And
then he sets forth that free grace which gave the redemption
that is in Christ Jesus (3:21-31). In chapter 4, he points to
Abraham as having understood, when he believed, that God
justified him freely by his grace and not for anything that he
had done.

Abraham had not only believed this, but something
more. "He believed in God, who gives life to the dead and
calls into existence the things that do not exist." The two
expressions are most significant and indicate the two
essential needs there are in the redemption of man in Christ
Jesus. There is the need of justification by faith, to restore
man to the favor of God. But he must also be quickened to a
new life. Just as justification is by faith alone, so is
regeneration. Christ died for our sins; he was raised again
out of, or through our justification.

In the first section (down to chapter 5:11) Paul deals
exclusively with the great thought of our justification. But
in the second section (5:12 to 8:39) he expounds that
wonderful union with Christ through faith, by which we
died with him, by which we live in him, and by which
through the Holy Spirit, we are freed, not only from the
punishment, but also from the power of sin and are enabled
to live the life of righteousness, obedience, and sanctification.

21 Dead with Christ
If we have died with Christ, we believe that we shall also live with him. (Rom 6:8)

The reason that God's children live so little in the power of the resurrection life of Christ is that they have so little understanding of or faith in their death with Christ. Paul says, "If we have died with Christ, we believe that we shall also live with him"; it is the knowledge and experience that assures us of the power of his resurrection in us. "The death he died he died to sin, once for all, but the life he lives he lives to God" (v. 10). It is only because and as we know that we are dead with him, that we can live with him.

On the strength of this, Paul now appeals to his readers. "So you also must consider yourselves dead to sin and alive to God in Christ Jesus" (v. 11). The words "consider yourselves" are a call to an act of bold and confident faith. Consider yourselves to be indeed dead unto sin, as much as Christ is, and alive to God in Christ Jesus. The word gives us a divine assurance of what we actually are and have in Christ. And this not as a truth that our minds can master and appropriate, but a reality which the Holy Spirit will reveal within us. In his power we accept our death with Christ on the cross as the power of our daily life.

Then we are able to accept and obey the command: "Let not sin therefore reign in your mortal bodies . . . but yield yourselves to God as men who have been brought from death to life . . . For sin will have no dominion over you" (vv. 12-14). "Having been set free from sin, [you] have become slaves of righteousness . . . so now yield your members to righteousness for sanctification . . . Now that you have been set free from sin and have become slaves of God, the return you get is sanctification" (vv. 18, 19, 22).

The whole chapter is a wonderful revelation of the deep meaning of its opening words: "How can we who died to sin still live in it?" Everything depends upon our acceptance of the divine assurance: if we died with Christ, as he died, and now lives to God, we too have the assurance that in him we have the power to live to God.

22 Dead to the Law

*You have died to the law through the body of Christ.
. . . We are discharged from the law, dead to that which held
us captive, so that we serve . . . in the new life of the Spirit.*
(Rom 7:4, 6)

The believer is not only dead to sin, but dead to the law. This
is a deeper truth, delivering us from a life of effort and
failure, and opening the way to the life in the power of the
Holy Spirit. "Thou shalt" is done away with; the power of
the Spirit takes its place. In the remainder of this chapter
(7:7-24) Paul describes the Christian as he still tries to obey
the law, but utterly fails. He experiences that "in him, that is
in his flesh, dwells no good thing." He finds that the law of
sin, notwithstanding his greatest efforts, continually brings
him into captivity, and compels the cry: "O wretched man
that I am, who shall deliver me from the body of this death?"
In the whole passage, it is everywhere, "I," without any
thought of the Spirit's help. It is only when he has uttered
his cry of despair that he is brought to see that he is no
longer under the law, but under the rule of the Holy Spirit
(8:1, 2). "There is therefore now no condemnation," such
as he had experienced in his attempt to obey the law, "to
them that are in Christ Jesus. For the law of the Spirit of life
in Christ Jesus has made me free from the law of sin and
death." As chapter 7 gives us the experience that leads to
being a captive under the power of sin, chapter 8 reveals the
experience of the life of a man in Christ Jesus, who has now
been freed from the law of sin and death. In the former we
have the life of the ordinary Christian doing his utmost to
keep the commandments of the law and to walk in God's
ways, but ever finding how much there is of failure and
shortcoming. In the latter we have the man who knows that
he is in Christ Jesus, dead to sin and alive to God, and by the
Spirit freed and kept free from the bondage of sin and of
death.

May we understand the deep meaning of Romans 7,
where we learn that in him, that is in his flesh, there is no
good thing, and that there is no deliverance from this state

but by yielding to the power of the Spirit freeing us from the power of bondage of the flesh, and so fulfilling the righteousness of the law in the power of the life of Christ!

23 The Flesh Condemned on the Cross
God has done what the law, weakened by the flesh, could not do: sending his own Son in the likeness of sinful flesh and for sin, he condemned sin in the flesh. (Rom 8:3)

In Romans 8:7 Paul writes, "The mind that is set on the flesh is hostile to God; it does not submit to God's law, indeed it cannot." Here Paul opens up the depth of sin that exists in the flesh. In chapter 7 he said that in the flesh there is no good thing. Here he goes deeper and tells us that the flesh is enmity against God; it hates God and his law. It was on this account that God condemned sin in the flesh on the cross; all the curse that is upon sin is upon the flesh in which sin dwells. As the believer understands this, he will cease from any attempt at perfecting in the flesh what is begun in the Spirit. The two are at deadly, irreconcilable enmity.

See how this lies at the very root of the true Christian life (vv. 3, 4): "God ... condemned sin in the flesh, in order that the just requirement of the law might be fulfilled in us, who walk not according to the flesh but according to the Spirit." All the requirements of God's law will be fulfilled, not in those who strive to keep and fulfill that law—a thing that is utterly impossible—but who walk by the Spirit and in his power live out the life that Christ won for us on the cross and imparted to us in the resurrection.

In me, that is in my flesh, in the old nature which I have from Adam, there dwells no good thing that can satisfy the eye of a holy God! That flesh can never, by any process of discipline, struggling, or prayer, be made better than it is! But the Son of God in the likeness of sinful flesh—in the form of a man—condemned sin on the cross. "There is now no condemnation to them which are in Christ Jesus, who walk, not after the flesh, but after the Spirit."

24 Jesus Christ and Him Crucified

I decided to know nothing among you except Jesus Christ and him crucified. And . . . my speech and my message were . . . in demonstration of the Spirit and of power. (1 Cor 2:2, 4)

This text is very often understood of Paul's purpose in his preaching to know nothing but Jesus Christ and him crucified. But it contains a far deeper thought. He speaks of his purpose, not only in the matter of his preaching, but in his whole spirit and life to prove how he in everything seeks to act in conformity to the crucified Christ. Thus he writes: "He was crucified in weakness, but lives by the power of God. For we are weak in him, but in dealing with you we shall live with him by the power of God" (2 Cor 13:4, 5). His whole ministry and conversation bore the mark of Christ's likeness—crucified through weakness, yet living by the power of God.

Just before the words of our text Paul had written: "The word of the cross is folly to those who are perishing, but to us who are being saved it is the power of God" (1:18-24). It was not only in his preaching, but in his whole disposition and deportment that he sought to act in harmony with that weakness in which Christ was crucified. He had so identified himself with the weakness of the cross, and its shame, that in his whole life and conduct he would prove that in everything he sought to show forth the likeness and the spirit of the crucified Jesus. Hence he says: "I was with you in weakness and in much fear and trembling" (2:3).

It is on this account that he spoke so strongly: "Christ did not send me to . . . preach the gospel, and not with eloquent wisdom, lest the cross of Christ be emptied of its power" (1:17); "My speech and my message were not in plausible words of wisdom, but in demonstration of the Spirit and of power" (2:4). Is this not the greatest reason why the power of God is so little manifested in the preaching of the gospel? Christ the crucified may be the subject of the preaching and yet there may be such confidence in human learning and eloquence that there is nothing to be seen of that likeness of the crucified Jesus which alone gives preaching its supernatural, its divine power.

May God help us to understand how the life of every minister and of every believer must bear the hallmark, the stamp of the sanctuary—nothing but Jesus Christ and him crucified.

25 Temperate in All Things
Every athlete exercises self-control in all things . . . I pommel my body and subdue it. (1 Cor 9:25, 27)

Paul here reminds us of the well-known principle that anyone competing for a prize in the public games is temperate and "exercises self-control in all things." Everything, however attractive, that might hinder in the race is given up or set aside. And this in order to obtain an earthly prize. Shall we, who strive for an incorruptible crown, not be temperate in all things that could in the very least prevent our following the Lord Jesus with an undivided heart?

Paul says, "I pommel my body and subdue it." He would allow nothing to hinder him. He tells us: "This one thing I do; I press towards the mark for the prize." No self-pleasing in eating and drinking, no comfort or ease, should for a moment keep him from showing the spirit of the cross in his daily life or from sacrificing all like his master. Read the following four passages which comprise his life-history: 1 Corinthians 4:11-13; 2 Corinthians 4:8-12; 6:4-10; 11:23-27. The cross was not only the theme of his preaching, but the rule of his life in all its details.

We need to pray that this disposition may be found in all Christians and preachers of the Gospel, through the power of the Holy Spirit. When the death of Christ works with power in the preacher, then Christ's life will be known among the people. Let us pray that the fellowship of the cross may regain its old place, and that God's children may obey the injunction, "Let this mind be in you that was in Christ Jesus." He humbled himself and became obedient unto the death of the cross. For, "if we have been united with him in a death like his, we shall certainly be united with him in a resurrection like his" (Rom 6:5).

26 The Dying of the Lord Jesus

Always carrying in the body the death of Jesus, so that the life of Jesus may also be manifested in our bodies. . . . So death is at work in us, but life in you. (2 Cor 4:10, 12)

Paul here is very bold in speaking of the intimate union that there was between Christ living in him, and the life he lived in the flesh, with all its suffering. He had spoken of his being crucified with Christ, and Christ living in him (Gal 2:20). Here he tells how he always carried in his body the death of Jesus; it was through this that the life of Jesus was manifested in his body. And he says that it was because the death of Christ was thus working in and through him that Christ's life could work in the Corinthians.

We often speak of abiding in Christ, but we forget that this means abiding in a *crucified* Christ. Many believers appear to think that when once they have claimed Christ's death in the fellowship of the cross and have counted themselves as crucified with him, that they may now consider it as past and done with. They do not understand that it is in the crucified Christ, and in the fellowship of his death, that they are to abide daily and unceasingly. The fellowship of the cross is to be our daily life and experience. The self-emptying of our Lord, his taking the form of a servant, his humbling himself and becoming obedient unto death, even the death of the cross—this mind that was in Christ is to be the disposition that marks our daily life.

"Always carrying in the body the death of Jesus." We are called to this as much as Paul. If we are indeed to live for the welfare of men around us, if we are to sacrifice our ease and pleasure to win souls for our Lord, it will be true of us as of Paul, that we are able to say: Death is at work in us, but life in those for whom we pray and labor. It is in the fellowship of the sufferings of Christ that the crucified Lord can live out and work out his life in us and through us.

The abiding in Christ Jesus, for which we have so often prayed and striven, is nothing less than the abiding of the Crucified in us and we in him.

27 The Cross and the Spirit

How much more shall the blood of Christ, who through the eternal Spirit offered himself without blemish to God, purify your conscience from dead works to serve the living God. (Heb 9:14)

The cross is Christ's highest glory. The glory which he received from the Father was entirely owing to his humbling himself to the death of the cross. "Therefore God highly exalted him." The greatest work which the Holy Spirit could ever do in the Son of God was when he enabled him to yield himself as a sacrifice and an offering. And the Holy Spirit can now do nothing greater or more glorious for us than to lead us into the fellowship and likeness of that crucified life of our Lord.

Is this not the reason our prayers for the mighty working of the Holy Spirit are not more abundantly answered? We have prayed too little that the Holy Spirit might glorify Christ in us in the fellowship and the conformity to his sufferings. The Spirit who led Christ to the cross is longing and is able to maintain in us the life of abiding in the crucified Jesus.

The Spirit and the cross are inseparable. The Spirit led Christ to the cross; the cross brought Christ to the throne to receive the fullness of the Spirit to impart to his people. The Spirit taught Peter to preach Christ crucified; through that preaching three thousand received the Spirit. In the preaching of the gospel, in the Christian life, as in Christ, so in us, the Spirit and the cross are inseparable. It is the sad lack of the mind and disposition of the crucified Christ, sacrificing self and the world to win life for the dying, that is one great cause of the feebleness of the Church. Let us beseech God fervently to teach us to say: We have been crucified with Christ; in him we have died to sin, "always carrying in the body the death of Jesus." So shall we be prepared for that fullness of the Spirit which the Father longs to bestow.

28 The Veil of the Flesh

Therefore, brethren, since we have confidence to enter the sanctuary by the blood of Jesus, by the new and living way which he opened for us through the curtain, that is, through his flesh. (Heb 10:19, 20)

In the temple there was a veil between the holy place and the most holy. At the altar in the court the blood of the sacrifice was sprinkled for forgiveness of sins. That gave the priest entrance into the holy place to offer God the incense as part of a holy worship. But into the most holy, behind the veil, the high priest alone might enter once a year. That veil was the type of sinful human nature; even though it had received the forgiveness of sin, full access and fellowship with God was impossible.

When Christ died, the veil was rent. Christ dedicated a new and living way to God through the rent veil of his flesh. This new way, by which we now can enter into the holiest of all, ever passes through the rent veil of the flesh. Every believer has "crucified the flesh with its passions and desires" (Gal 5:24). Every step on the new and living way for entering into God's holy presence maintains the fellowship with the cross of Christ. The rent veil of the flesh refers not only to Christ and his sufferings, but to our experience in the likeness of his sufferings.

This is why many Christians have never attained close fellowship with God. They have never yielded the flesh as an accursed thing to the condemnation of the cross. They desire to enter into the holiest of all, and yet allow the flesh with its desires and pleasures to rule over them. May God help us to understand, in the power of the Holy Spirit, that Christ has called us to hate our life, to lose our life, to be dead with him to sin that we may live to God with him. There is no way to a full, abiding fellowship with God, but through the rent veil of the flesh, through a life with the flesh crucified in Christ Jesus. Praise God that the Holy Spirit continually dwells in us to keep the flesh in its place of crucifixion and condemnation, and to give us the abiding victory over all temptations.

29 Looking to Jesus

Let us run with perseverance the race that is set before us, looking to Jesus the pioneer and perfecter of our faith, who for the joy that was set before him endured the cross, despising the shame. (Heb 12:1, 2)

In running a race the eye and heart are ever set upon the goal and the prize. The Christian is here called to keep his eye fixed on Jesus enduring the cross, as the one object of imitation and desire. Throughout our whole life we are to be animated by his Spirit as he bore the cross. This was the way that led to the throne and the glory of God. This is the new and living way which he opened for us through the veil of the flesh. It is as we study and realize that it was for his bearing the cross that God so highly exalted him, that we shall walk in his footsteps, bearing our cross after him with the flesh condemned and crucified.

The impotence of the Church is greatly due to the fact that this cross-bearing mind of Jesus is so little preached and practiced. Most Christians think that as long as they do not commit actual sin, they are free to possess and enjoy as much of the world as they please. There is so little insight into the deep truth that the world, and the flesh that loves the world, is enmity with God. Hence many Christians seek and pray for years for conformity to the image of Jesus, and yet fail so entirely. They do not know, and do not seek with the whole heart to know, what it is to die to self and the world.

It was for the joy set before him that Christ endured the cross—the joy of pleasing and glorifying the Father, the joy of loving and winning souls for himself. We need a new crusade with the proclamation: This is the will of God, that as Christ found his highest happiness and received from the Father the fullness of the Spirit to pour down on his people, through his endurance of the cross, so it is only in our fellowship of the cross that we can really become conformed to the image of God's Son. As believers awaken to this truth and run the race looking to the crucified Jesus, they will receive power to win for Christ the souls he has purchased on the cross.

30 Without the Gate

The bodies of those animals whose blood is brought into the sanctuary by the high priest as a sacrifice for sin are burned outside the camp. So Jesus also suffered outside the gate in order to sanctify the people through his own blood. Therefore let us go forth to him outside the camp, and bear the abuse he endured. (Heb 13:11-13)

The blood of the sin offering was brought into the Holy Place; the body of the sacrifice was burned outside the camp. Even so with Christ, his blood was presented to the Father; but his body was cast out as an accursed thing, outside the camp.

And so we read in Hebrews 10: "Let us enter into the Holy Place by the blood of Jesus." And in our text: "Let us go forth to him outside the camp, and bear the abuse he endured." The deeper my insight into the boldness which his blood gives me in God's presence, the greater the joy with which I may enter the Holy Place. And the deeper my insight into the shame of the cross which he bore on my behalf outside the camp, the more willing shall I be, in the fellowship of his cross, to follow him outside the camp, bearing his abuse.

Many Christians love to hear of the boldness with which we can enter into the Holy Place through his blood, yet have little desire for the fellowship of his abuse. They are unwilling to separate themselves from the world with the same boldness with which they think to enter the sanctuary. The Christian suffers inconceivable loss when he thinks of entering into the Holy Place in faith and prayer, and then feels himself free to enjoy the friendship of the world, so long as he does nothing actually sinful. But the Word of God has said: "The friendship of the world is enmity against God." "Love not the world, neither the things that are in the world; if any man love the world, the love of the Father is not in him." "Be not conformed to this world."

To be a follower of Christ implies a heart given up to testify for Christ in the midst of the world, if by any means some may be won. To follow Christ means to be like him in his love of the cross and his willingness to sacrifice self that the Father may be glorified and men saved.

Lord, teach me what it means to follow you outside the camp, bearing your abuse, and so witness to your holy redeeming love, as it embraces those who are in the world to win them back to the Father. Lord, let the spirit and the love that was in you be in me too, that I may at any cost seek to win the souls for whom you died.

Other Books of Interest

A Lamp for My Feet
The Bible's Light for Daily Living
Elisabeth Elliot

Devotions that reflect this outstanding Christian woman's personal encounters with Scripture. *$9.95* (hardcover)

Chosen Vessels
Portraits of Ten Outstanding Christian Men
Edited by Charles Turner

Men like Malcolm Muggeridge, J.I. Packer, Charles Colson, Phillip Keller, and Philip Yancey write about great Christian men like William Wilberforce, Alexander Solzhenitsyn, C.S. Lewis, Paul Brand, and many more. *$10.95* (hardcover)

Only a Prayer Away
John Guest

A month-long course in prayer with a lesson for each of twenty-eight days. Excellent for individual or group use. Foreword by R.C. Sproul. *$5.95* (hardcover)